ARMS CONTROL FACT BOOK

Compiled by

Dennis Menos

McFarland & Company, Inc., Publishers
Jefferson, North Carolina, and London

To Anne-Marie and her generation

Library of Congress Cataloging in Publication Data

Menos, Dennis, 1924–
  Arms control fact book.

  Bibliography: p.
  Includes index.
  1. Arms Control. 2. Nuclear arms control.
I. Title.
JX1974.M44 1985   327.1'74   84-43243

ISBN 0-89950-158-3 (alk. paper)

Printed in the United States of America

McFarland   Box 611   Jefferson NC 28640

Table of Contents

In encyclopedic format: concise descriptions of significant factors, concepts, and items of the U.S. and international structure for arms control, including agreements and treaties in force, ongoing negotiations and conferences, weapon systems, public interest topics, jargon, historical events, etc.

About 50 agencies, institutes, committees, associations, foundations, centers, councils, and other groups: address, description, purpose, activities, publications

Preface

Since detonation, in the summer of 1945, of the first nuclear device, the field of arms control has grown steadily in urgency and complexity. It is now in the very center of international debate on the future of mankind and, unquestionably, the paramount issue of our day.

In preparing this book, I had but one purpose in mind: to help the layman understand the basic issues underlying arms control, its accomplishments to date, and the challenges for the future. In so doing, I tried to use clear nontechnical language, and have kept the text intentionally free of complex descriptions on negotiating positions or details of nuclear technologies driving the arms race. Arms control, however, encompasses much more than formal negotiations, treaties, and advanced weapon systems. It includes also millions of people in the United States and abroad who are dedicated to arresting the arms race and preventing a nuclear holocaust. It is for this reason, and to recognize their efforts, that a part of the book is devoted to the major U.S. and foreign organizations which are active in arms control and disarmament.

Some aspects of arms control are extremely controversial. Examples include, the Nuclear Freeze concept, the "Strategic Defense Initiative" (STAR WARS), and the Soviet record on arms treaty compliance. In presenting these subjects in Part I of the book, I withheld my personal views, choosing instead to discuss both sides of the particular issue. I believe this to be a good policy, even though at times, it deprives the reader of a definitive "answer" to his/her question.

Dennis Menos
January 1985

Part I
Substantive Data

ABM System. See **Ballistic Missile Defense (BMD)**.

Accidental Attack. In the nuclear age, the term is used to describe an unintended nuclear attack, i.e. one which occurs without deliberate design on the part of the nation from whose territory it is launched. Such an attack could result from the mechanical failure of a weapon, a human error, or unauthorized action by a subordinate officer.

The likelihood that an accidental nuclear attack will ever occur is extremely low, primarily due to the ever-increasing number and sophistication of the precautions adopted by the nuclear-weapon nations. In the United States (and probably also in the Soviet Union) these precautions require that two persons perform the various actions which must be carried out prior to arming and delivering a nuclear weapon. The process requires also the knowledge of highly secure codes available only to a few carefully selected members of the armed forces. Additional precautions guard against the accidental detonation of the weapons themselves during training, or because of exposure to heat, blast, or radiation.

Accidents Measures Agreement. This bilateral agreement between the United States and the Soviet Union on "Measures to Reduce the Risk of Outbreak of Nuclear War," was signed in Washington, DC, on September 30, 1971.

Under the terms of the agreement, each party undertakes to maintain and improve its organizational and technical arrangements to guard against the accidental or unauthorized use of nuclear weapons under its control. The parties, furthermore, pledge to notify each other immediately in the event of:
- an accidental, unauthorized, or unexplained incident involving a possible detonation of a nuclear weapon;
- the detection by their missile warning systems of unidentified objects; and

1

• any planned missile launching beyond their national territory and in the direction of the other party.

The agreement concludes by requiring that the "Hot Line" be utilized for urgent communications in all such cases or in situations requiring prompt clarification.

Agency for the Prohibition of Nuclear Weapons in Latin America. This agency was established by the Latin America Nuclear Free Zone Treaty to ensure compliance with the treaty obligations. Agency headquarters are in Mexico City.

The agency's principal administrative organs include a General Conference, a Council and a Secretariat. The General Conference meets in regular session every two years. Participants include:
• all states which are signatories to the basic treaty;
• "partial parties" (Argentina, Brazil, Chile, the People's Republic of China, France, Netherlands, United States, United Kingdom and the Soviet Union);
• several non-parties; and
• representatives of the U.N., the IAEA, and of other international organizations concerned with issues of arms control.

Antarctic Treaty. The Antarctic Treaty is the earliest of the post-World War II arms limitation agreements. Signed on December 1, 1959, it internationalizes and demilitarizes the Antarctic continent and provides for its cooperative exploration and future use. The treaty is also noteworthy in that it gives each signatory nation on-site inspection rights for all stations, installations, and equipment located in Antarctica.

The treaty provides that Antarctica shall be used for peaceful purposes only. It specifically prohibits "any measures of a military nature, such as the establishment of military bases and fortifications, the carrying out of military maneuvers, as well as the testing of any type of weapons." Nuclear weapons and the disposal of radioactive waste material are especially prohibited. All contracting parties have the right to designate observers and to carry out inspections, including aerial surveillance, in all areas of Antarctica.

Anti-Satellite Weapons. As the name implies, anti-satellite (ASAT) weapons are designed to track and destroy satellites. A large number of possibilities exist for accomplishing this mission, although specific weapons in each case remain to be developed. Maneuvering spacecraft are probably the most effective means for reaching and destroying satellites. Others include direct interceptors, energy weapons such as lasers and particle beams, and electronic counter-measures of sufficient power to damage and interrupt key satellite functions.

As of this writing, the Soviet Union has an ASAT system while the United States is on the verge of developing one. The Soviet system is by all accounts rather elementary. Launched by a space booster, it is placed into orbit near an intended victim, and on order from a ground station explodes, shattering the target satellite with a shower of fragments. The system is apparently effective in low orbits only. In contrast, the United States system presently under development is far more sophisticated. It consists of a miniature homing device, capable of tracking and destroying enemy satellites with near-perfect accuracy. The fact that the U.S. weapon could be launched from high-flying F-15 fighter planes, makes it, so the critics charge, far more destabilizing than its Soviet counterpart. Unlike the Soviet system, which can be tracked as it is launched, the U.S. weapon could strike without warning from fighter planes anywhere in the world.

The Reagan Administration is pursuing development of the ASAT weapon with great urgency. The weapon itself was tested successfully in January 1984 and again in November 1984, and plans are under way to test it next against a satellite target. However, there is great opposition in the Congress to the latter test, as evidenced by a series of amendments to the FY 1985 Defense authorization bill which prohibit ASAT testing against objects in space prior to March 1, 1985. After that date, ASAT weapons tests against objects in space can be conducted, provided that the President certifies that he is bargaining with the Soviets in "good faith" toward an arms control agreement.

Arms Control. The term embraces all activities which are designed to limit, control, reduce, or eliminate the armed forces and armaments of nations under international agreement. Purpose, of course, is to strengthen international peace and stability and to lessen the likelihood of nuclear war. In the United States, the term is not synonymous with "disarmament"; in the United Nations arena, how-ever, the opposite is true and both terms are used interchangeably.

The U.S. and the Soviet arms control policies have much in common: both nations are seeking to reduce the risk of nuclear war by means of agreements which reduce armaments, strengthen deterrence, and control crisis escalation. Enormous differences, however, exist on the paths which these nations have chosen to implement their policy. The dearth of arms control agreements during the past decade, and the ever-increasing arms race, are obvious results of these differences.

Arms control agreements negotiated with the Soviet Union since World War II, and placed into effect, include the three "Hot Line" agreements, SALT I, and agreements to "control accidents" and to "prevent a nuclear war." Three signed accords (including SALT II) are in "hold" status, but negotiations in three areas are expected to be resumed soon (see **Umbrella Talks**). Additionally, the United States and the Soviet Union are signatories to ten international arms control agreements negotiated under U.N. auspices.

Arms Control and Disarmament Act. This Act was enacted in 1961 during the presidency of J.F. Kennedy. Its basic purpose was to create the Arms Control and Disarmament Agency (ACDA), the government's central organization for arms control and disarmament policy. The Act has been amended repeatedly as part of the annual congressional appropriations process, the latest amendment being dated October 15, 1982.

The Act defines the ultimate goal of the United States as "a world free from the scourge of war and the dangers and burdens of armaments." However, it also cautions that arms control and disarmament policy must be consistent with national security policy as a whole.

Three primary functions are assigned to ACDA in the Act: research for arms control and disarmament policy formulation; preparation for and management of U.S. participation in arms control and disarmament negotiations; and dissemination of public information in the field.

Section 37 of the Act deals specifically with the verification of arms control agreements. It declares that "adequate verification of compliance should be an indispensable part of any international arms control agreement."

Arms Control and Disarmament Agency (ACDA). ACDA was established by statute in 1961 as an independent agency of the Executive Branch reporting directly to the President. It is assigned primary responsibility within the Federal Government for the development and negotiation of international agreements to reduce and control nuclear arms.

In the performance of its duties, ACDA works closely with the National Security Council Staff, the Departments of State and Defense, and the U.S. foreign intelligence community. The agency performs a broad range of functions: it manages the United States participation in arms control and disarmament negotiations; leads the U.S. delegations to most such forums; and plays the lead role in the preparation and coordination of U.S. negotiating positions. All activities are carried out as an integral component of overall U.S. foreign and national security policy.

The agency's total staff consists of 180 full-time employees and its annual budget is approximately 17 million dollars. Four agency publications are especially noteworthy:

- *ACDA Annual Report* (this is the agency's annual report to the Congress; it is released each January).
- *Arms Control and Disarmament Agreements* (contains texts of all arms control and disarmament agreements enacted since World War II).
- *Documents on Disarmament* (contains excerpts from all key arms control and disarmament documents published during the year).
- *Arms Control Impact Statements* (this publication is submitted to the Congress each fiscal year, in compliance with Section 36 of the Arms Control and Disarmament Act).

Arms-Treaty Compliance. Few arms control issues evoke greater controversy than arms-treaty compliance. To millions of Americans, the Soviets are clearly violating their arms control commitments and in the process gaining a distinct military advantage over the United States. To others, the Soviet violations are hardly devastating and result from either ambiguities in the language of agreements or inadequacies in intelligence data upon which to base proper evaluations of the reported infractions.

Most serious observers agree that from an overall perspective, the arms control agreements enacted thus far have held quite well. Certainly, the United States has not tried to openly violate any of the existing agreements and, from all indications, neither have the Soviets. True, there have been questionable activities on both sides, unintentional violations, possibly even some intentional infractions, but none of them have been at a scale large enough to result in a major strategic breakthrough to either side because of arms control cheating.

Through the years, the governments of the United States and of the Soviet Union have accused each other, repeatedly, of arms control violations. To a great extent, these mutual recriminations have been politically motivated or have been designed as exercises in public relations. Actually, there has been considerable parallelism between the U.S. and Soviet charges. The United States has accused the Soviets, for instance, of building a nationwide ABM system in violation of the ABM Treaty, citing the erection of a large radar in Krasnoyarsk as evidence. The Soviets have responded by charging that President

Reagan's "Strategic Defense Initiative" is a mere euphemism for an ABM defense system which the United States is developing. The United States has accused the Soviets of using deliberate concealment to impede verification by National Technical Means; they responded by reviving an old issue, the sheltering of the Titan and Minuteman silos during upgrading, a practice which the United States abandoned years ago. The United States has charged that the development by the Soviet Union of two different ICBM systems (the SS-X-24 and SS-X-25) is in clear violation of the limitations imposed by the SALT II agreement, a charge repeated by the Soviet Union with regard to the U.S. development of two parallel ICBM systems (the MX and the Midgetman). Finally, both the United States and the Soviet Union have accused each other of testing at yields exceeding 150 KT, thus violating the Threshold Test Ban Treaty.

Assured Destruction Strategy. U.S. strategy of deterrence, first articulated by former Secretary of Defense Robert S. McNamara. Strategy remained in effect throughout the 1960s and 70s, i.e. the period during which the United States enjoyed strategic nuclear superiority over the Soviet Union. The strategy required that the United States maintain strategic nuclear forces of such size, flexibility, survivability and control, so as to enable it to absorb a Soviet first strike and still possess sufficient strength to inflict "unacceptable damage" on the Soviet Union in a retaliatory attack. "Unacceptable damage" was defined as the destruction of one-third of the Soviet population, two-thirds of its industry, and approximately 200 of its major cities.

The explosive growth of the Soviet strategic forces since the mid-1970s has required that "Assured Destruction" be updated as a basic strategy. Mutual Assured Destruction (MAD) is the strategy of deterrence now being employed. It specifies that the principal use of U.S. nuclear forces is to deter the other (Soviet) side from using its nuclear forces. Both nations possess an "assured destruction" capability.

Ballistic Missile Defense (BMD). A defensive system which destroys incoming ballistic missiles or their warheads. The Soviet Union has a BMD system deployed around Moscow. The United States has no such system; however, the "Strategic Defense Initiative" (SDI) is designed to eventually build an effective nationwide strategic defense against ballistic missiles. The term "anti-ballistic missile system" or "ABM" is used often interchangeably with BMD.

Binary Weapons. These are highly toxic weapons created from the mixture of two nonlethal chemicals. The mixture takes place during the flight of a missile, shell or bomb in which the constituent gasses are loaded. Since binary nerve gas weapons do not become lethal until the mixture of their components in flight, they can be stored and handled more easily than other toxic gasses.

Biological Weapons Convention. This convention on the "Prohibition of the Development, Production and Stockpiling of Bacteriological (Biological) and Toxin Weapons and on their Destruction" was signed in Washington, London, and Moscow on April 10, 1972. To date, a total of 98 nations have deposited documents of accession and an additional 30 have signed the Convention. France and the People's Republic of China, however, have refused to join for fear that the Convention might weaken the Geneva Convention on the use of chemical weapons.

Under the terms of the convention, each party undertakes not to develop, produce, stockpile or otherwise acquire or retain: (a) microbial or other biological agents, or toxins, of types and in quantities that have no justification for prophylactic, protective, or other peaceful purposes; and (b) weapons, equipment or means of delivery designed to use such agents or toxins for hostile purposes or in armed conflict. Additionally, each party undertakes to destroy, or to divert for peaceful purposes, as soon as possible, but not later than nine months after the entry into force of the convention, all "biological" weapons in its possession.

Build-down of Nuclear Forces. This is a bipartisan Congressional initiative conceived in February 1983 by Senators Nunn and Cohen. It proposes reductions in the nuclear arsenals of the superpowers by means of a fairly simple formula: the destruction of two nuclear warheads for each new warhead deployed. The concept enjoys Presidential support and was incorporated into the U.S. negotiating position in the now suspended Strategic Arms Reduction Talks (START).

B-1B Bomber. This is a long-range combat aircraft designed as a replacement for the aging B-52 bomber. The plane's primary mission is that of a penetrating bomber, but it is capable also of supporting other forms of warfare (e.g. tactical land combat, cruise missile launchings, theater nuclear operations, and naval warfare). The B-1B is being built using many of the components originally designed for the B-1A. The latter aircraft was cancelled in 1977 by President Carter as "not necessary." A total of 100 B-1B bombers are planned by 1988 at an estimated cost of over $29 billion.

Production of the B-1B was ordered by President Reagan late in

1981. Production is on schedule, with the initial increment of 15 aircraft expected to be delivered to the Strategic Air Command in October 1986. As of this writing, flight testing is underway of the first production model rolled out of assembly in September 1984.

Supporters of the B-1B argue that a critical need exists to replace the aging B-52 bomber until the "Stealth" aircraft is developed. Also, that much of the B-1B airframe and electronic technology is already available and can be readily used to strengthen the U.S. deterrent. Critics respond that the advent of cruise missiles has made manned bombers less important. This, and the ever-increasing Soviet air defense capabilities, make it unwise to pursue the B-1B instead of the "Stealth" bomber.

Central Intelligence Agency (CIA) (Role in Arms Control). In fulfilling its role as the nation's senior intelligence organization, the CIA participates actively in all aspects of arms control policy and implementation. The main thrust of this activity, of course, is in the area of verification, more specifically the U.S. ability to verify the provisions of arms control agreements and proposals. The specific CIA activities under this program are obviously classified, because of the intelligence sources and methods used in the collection and analysis of data. In carrying out its function, the CIA relies heavily on several other members of the U.S. foreign intelligence community, especially the National Security Agency and the Defense Intelligence Agency.

Cessation of the Nuclear Arms Race. There is general consensus in the international arena on the need to end the nuclear arms race. With no nation obviously favoring a nuclear arms race, debate has centered on the specific measures for accomplishing this objective.

Spearheading the effort are several Third World nations and, to an extent, the People's Republic of China. In their view, the existence of nuclear weapons in the arsenals of a handful of powers threatens the security of the entire world. It is politically and morally unjustified, they claim, that the future of mankind should be held hostage to the security arrangements of the nuclear-weapons states. They suggest a "nuclear freeze" as a prerequisite to nuclear disarmament. See also **Five-Continent Peace Initiative.**

The two superpowers differ sharply on the means for accomplishing the objective. The Soviet proposal is for the elimination of all nuclear stockpiles by means of a stage-by-stage nuclear destruction program. The existing nuclear balance would remain undisturbed while nuclear stocks are being eliminated. The United States supports progress through the negotiation of verifiable arms control agreements. It is opposed to the "nuclear freeze" idea as a detraction from other more serious arms control efforts currently under way.

Chemical Weapons. Chemical weapons were used extensively during World War I, and according to official reports, casualties numbered approximately 1,300,000 of which about 100,000 were fatal.

Rapid scientific and technological advances during the past three decades have increased the destructive potential of chemical agents. Principal types available in the military arsenals of nations include:

- Nerve agents: Are colorless, odorless, and tasteless. They poison the nervous system, disrupt vital functions, and kill quickly.
- Blister agents: Are oily liquids which burn and blister the skin. They have also general toxic effects.
- Choking agents: They irritate and severely injure lungs and breathing ability.
- Psycho-chemicals: Cause temporary mental disturbances, and confuse and demoralize combatants.

More recent developments include binary weapons, created from the formation of nonlethal constituents. The chemical reaction of binary weapons occurs only during the flight of the munition to its target.

Chemical Weapons Control. International concern has long been directed toward the need to effect a complete prohibition of chemical weapons. An important step toward their elimination was taken shortly after World War I with the conclusion of the Geneva Convention of 1925. However, as significant as this early arms control measure was, it provided only for part of the solution, i.e. it outlawed the "use" only of chemical weapons, not their production or stockpiling. Accordingly, chemical weapons continue to be maintained in the arsenals of many nations.

To help ensure that chemical weapons will never be used, a complete and effective prohibition in their development, production, and stockpiling is being sought, to include the destruction of existing stockpiles. The goal is being pursued by the Conference on Disarmament through a formally established Working Group. Concurrently, the United States and Soviet Union have been conducting bilateral discussions on this issue for nearly seven years. Serious differences remain, especially on key verification issues:

- The United States favors on-site verification on a continuous basis. The Soviet Union, at most, will agree to on-site inspection as a result of a challenge.
- The exact procedures to be followed in the disposition of existing stockpiles remain to be developed. Concern exists that chemicals required for law enforcement purposes might be upgraded surreptitiously for military use.
- The disposition of plants currently producing chemical weapons is a related consideration. Some nations favor their destruction; others suggest their conversion to civilian use. Dual-mission plants (i.e. those which produce chemical weapons as well as "permitted chemicals") present special disposition and verification problems.

In April 1984, the United States unveiled a draft treaty on chemical weapons control before the Conference on Disarmament. The draft sought to resolve many of the above verification issues. The Soviet Union, however, has rejected the United States proposal as a "setback in the negotiations."

Chinese Nuclear Forces. Although technically capable of striking the continental U.S. as well as Soviet Siberia, the People's Republic of China's strategic offensive forces are relatively small and unsophisticated. China's intermediate-range nuclear force, however is significant both numerically and with respect to the targets it can reach. The Chinese submarine-launched ballistic missiles program, although progressing, is years away from reaching operational deployment status.

Civil Defense. This term embraces all activities designed to protect a nation's civil population against the ravages of nuclear war, including the construction of shelters, the evacuation of urban populations, emergency communications, and educational activities.

U.S. civil defense programs have traditionally been limited in scope, partly due to the realization that protection against a massive nuclear attack is impossible. In contrast, the Soviet Union is pursuing a fairly extensive civil defense program predicated on protecting its leadership, the work force at key economic facilities, and the general population (in that order) from the effects of nuclear attack. Shelters are already available for approximately 10% of the Soviet urban population.

Through the years, military strategists in the West have differed over the worth of civil defense preparations in a nuclear war environment. Supporters maintain that civil defense can contribute significantly to crisis management by reducing the loss of human life, especially in nuclear confrontations involving the detonation of a few weapons only. Opponents argue that civil defense preparations actually increase the likelihood of nuclear war, by giving a nation a false sense of security and prompting its leadership to assume risks which it would otherwise not take.

Comprehensive Program of Disarmament. The need for a "Comprehensive Program of Disarmament" (i.e. a Master Plan for Disarmament) has been debated extensively over the past decade in various arms control/disarmament forums, especially within the Conference on Disarmament and at the Special Sessions on Disarmament of the United Nations General Assembly. Progress has been slow, because of persisting major differences over the scope and timing of the proposed program.

As envisioned by a Working Group of the Conference on Disarmament which serves as the focal point for the issue, the "program" will have three objectives: to eliminate the danger of nuclear war; to halt and reverse the arms race (both nuclear and conventional); and to lead mankind to general and complete disarmament under effective international control. A very large number of actions would be required to accomplish these objectives, such as the prevention of the use of force in international relations, the reduction of military budgets, and the elimination and destruction of all nuclear, biological, and radiological weapon stocks.

Comprehensive Test Ban Treaty. A treaty imposing a comprehensive ban on nuclear explosions has been on the international agenda since the mid-1950s. It has been an arms control goal of every American administration since that of President Eisenhower and has been a prime objective of the United Nations. Deliberations toward this treaty have been held in two forums: within the framework of the Conference on Disarmament (and its predecessor organizations in Geneva); and between representatives of the Soviet Union, the United Kingdom, and the United States. (The latter negotiations were suspended by the United States in July 1982).

As presently envisioned, the Comprehensive Test Ban Treaty (CTBT) will prohibit all nuclear tests, will have a fixed duration, and will enter into force when a specified number of states—including the United States, the United Kingdom, and the Soviet Union—have ratified it. A protocol, which will be an integral part of the treaty, will establish a moratorium on nuclear explosions for peaceful purposes. It will remain in effect until an agreed method can be found to preclude the acquisition of military benefits from nuclear explosions for peaceful purposes.

Certain of the key provisions of the treaty have already been agreed upon, but much work remains on the issues of compliance and verification of underground nuclear tests. Technology, the United States insists, does not allow discrimination between small underground nuclear explosions and seismic events. Accordingly, only a verification system consisting of control points and supplemented by the physical inspection of suspected sites can provide assurance that the provisions of the treaty are not being violated. The Soviet Union is strongly opposed to any verification system which would permit inspectors to enter Soviet territory, except possibly by "invitation" and under some very vague and unspecified conditions.

Conference on Confidence and Security Building Measures. Technically, this is the Conference on Confidence and Security Building of the European Disarmament Conference. It has been meeting in Stockholm since January 16, 1984 with representatives of thirty-five nations in attendance. All nations of Europe are represented (except Albania), plus the United States and Canada. The conference is an outgrowth of the "Review" CSCE meeting recently completed in Madrid. It seeks ways to reduce the risk of war in Europe.

Both NATO and the Warsaw Pact nations have presented proposals before the conference. The NATO plan, tabled in January 1984, calls for specific confidence and security building measures that would reduce: the risk of surprise attack; war by miscalculation; the use of force for political intimidation; and problems of communications in a potential crisis. The Warsaw Pact proposal contains both large-scale political measures (such as the nonuse of force, no first use of nuclear weapons, and adoption of nuclear-weapon free zones) and detailed confidence-building measures, such as limitations in the scope of military exercises and advance notification of large-scale military maneuvers. Neutral and nonaligned nations have also presented proposals, dealing with the establishment of nuclear-free zones in the Balkans, the Baltic, the Scandinavian region, and possibly also in Central Europe.

Conference on Disarmament. Formerly the Committee on Disarmament, this is the principal international body dealing with arms control and disarmament issues. It consists of forty nations active in the disarmament field, including the five major nuclear-weapon powers: the United States, the United Kingdom, France, the People's Republic of China, and the Soviet Union.

The Conference is an autonomous body linked, however, organizationally to the United Nations through its Secretary-General who serves as the personal representative of his United Nations counterpart. The presidency of the Conference rotates on a monthly basis among its member states and decisions are taken by consensus. Meetings are held in Geneva in the spring and summer of each year.

The following issues were considered by the Conference during its 1984 sessions:

- Verification and compliance issues hindering the final enactment of a Comprehensive Nuclear Test Ban Treaty.
- Cessation of the nuclear arms race and prevention of nuclear war.
- Negotiation of an international convention banning the development, production and stockpiling of chemical weapons.
- Prevention of an arms race in outer space.
- Provision of assurances of nonuse of nuclear weapons against nonnuclear weapon states ("negative security assurances").
- Development of a *Comprehensive Program of Disarmament*.
- Conclusion of a treaty prohibiting the development, production, stockpiling, and use of radiological weapons.

Predecessor organizations of the Conference on Disarmament were: the Committee on Disarmament (1968–1984); the Conference of the Eighteen-Nation Committee on Disarmament (1962–1968); and the Conference of the Ten-Nation Committee on Disarmament (1959–1962). The present Conference is in the process of considering a proposal for the expansion of its membership from forty to forty-four states.

Conference on Security and Cooperation in Europe (CSCE). This conference, with thiry-five nations participating, met in Helsinki over a period of several years. Its Final Act covers a wide range of issues of concern to the European continent, with security, interstate relations, and human rights being the most important.

Within a year of the conclusion of the Helsinki Conference a "Review" CSCE meeting was held in Madrid. Its purpose was to sustain the CSCE Final Act and to further the spirit of European cooperation prevalent in Helsinki. Security discussions at Madrid led to an agreement for a European Disarmament Conference, to be preceded, however, by a Conference on Confidence and Security Building Measures. Success at this preparatory conference (begun in Stockholm on January 16, 1984) is essential before the broader European Disarmament Conference is convened.

Confidence Building Measures. This term is applied to measures designed to demonstrate a nation's nonbelligerent intent, especially for activities (such as troop movements) which are likely to be misinterpreted by an opponent. Examples of such measures include advance notification of military exercises, the use of "hot lines" for communications during crises, and improved observation and inspection procedures.

The United States is a strong supporter of confidence building measures as a prerequisite to arms control agreements. It considers such measures to be effective in reducing the risk of surprise attack and the threat of war by accident or miscalculation. During the past decade, the Soviet Union has also been promoting confidence building measures, especially as regard the NATO and Warsaw Pact forces in central Europe.

Measures to dispel distrust and to build confidence among nations have been known through the ages. History is full of examples of gestures made by world leaders to prove peaceful intentions. Confidence building measures contribute toward reducing or eliminating the causes of distrust, fear, tensions and hostilities.

Countercity. This is a strategic doctrine for the use of nuclear weapons in wartime. Countercity relies primarily on the destruction of an opponent's civilian and economic centers as a means of achieving victory. Three reasons are cited by supporters as justifying countercity targeting: large urban areas are centers of government, industry, and transportation, and as such, represent the backbone of a nation's strength; cities are easy targets to locate and destroy; under present technology and barring spectacular breakthroughs in defensive systems, large urban areas cannot be defended against a missile attack.

The United States has never formally subscribed to the countercity doctrine, and it is highly unlikely that, considering American moral values, countercity would ever be utilized except as a very last resort in a national "survive or perish" situation. The Soviets, however, appear to favor (if not adhere to) a countercity strategy. Repeatedly, their military authors and tacticians have expressed the view that a nuclear war between the superpowers will be a "total" war, with the destruction of civilian targets being a logical consequence.

Counterforce. This is a strategic doctrine for the use of nuclear weapons in wartime. Counterforce relies on the destruction of an opponent's military forces and war-making potential as a means of achieving victory. Thus, targets of a counterforce strike would include ICBM silos, submarine bases, strategic airports and nuclear weapon storage areas, but not urban centers or populations. The civilian population of a belligerent nation would not become involved in the conflict, and the nation with the largest, most protected, and better directed nuclear forces would win. The doctrine was first declared by former Secretary of Defense Robert S. McNamara as an incentive to the Soviets to withhold nuclear attacks on American cities in the event of a U.S.–Soviet confrontation.

Although ostensibly designed to spare human life, the counterforce doctrine has been severely criticized by arms control advocates, as making the use of nuclear weapons more palatable. Considering the large number (estimated to be in the thousands) and hardening of counterforce targets, and their location generally near large urban centers, it hardly seems possible that a counterforce strike (no matter how limited) can spare human life.

In their writings, Soviet military strategists have generally expressed opposition to the counterforce doctrine, as not consistent with their national interests. Officially, the United States is also opposed to counterforce, because it reduces the number of nuclear options available to the President in the event of military conflict.

Cruise Missiles. Cruise missiles are subsonic, pilotless airplanes, patterned after the German V-1 buzz bombs of World War II. They are small, relatively inexpensive to build, and can be launched from a great variety of platforms. Flying at heights of not more than 100 feet, they escape radar detection, and attack their targets with pinpoint accuracy. Their range of operations usually averages 2,000 kilometers.

Cruise missiles are either nuclear-armed or conventional, with no outward differences in appearance. It is for this reason, and because their small size makes them easy to conceal, that arms control activists refer to them as the "nightmare" weapon, the one most likely to destabilize the present nuclear balance. Both the United States and the Soviet Union are producing cruise missiles in quantity and are deploying them with their strategic forces.

On the United States side, ground-launched cruise missiles (GLCMs) are presently being deployed in western Europe under the "Dual Track" decision of December 1979 (a total of 464 Tomahawk cruise missiles are planned for deployment, with ranges able to reach Soviet territory). Sea-launched cruise missiles (SLCMs) are just now entering the force, initially on surface ships and later on submarines. The Navy is reportedly planning to acquire 4,000 cruise missiles, one-fourth of them nuclear-armed. Air-launched cruise missiles (ALCMs) are already deployed on board B-52 bombers, with plans calling for their deployment also on board the B-1B bomber.

Deliberate Concealment. The term refers to the use of camouflage, deception, or other deliberate concealment to impede verification by National Technical Means (NTM). Recent arms control agreements, most notably SALT I and II, prohibit "deliberate concealment" whenever such activity is likely to impede verification.

The issue is especially critical with regard to the denial of telemetry, the electronic signals emitted during missile tests. Such telemetry often provides the first reliable information on a new weapon system and its characteristics. Accordingly, monitoring of telemetry is an important aspect of arms control verification.

The superpowers have repeatedly accused each other of "deliberate concealment." The United States charges have concerned Soviet encryption practices of missile test telemetry, an accusation denied by the Soviets. The Soviet charges have centered on a U.S. practice (now abandoned) of placing shelters over the Minuteman and Titan missiles sites during silo hardening and weapon modification operations. See also **Arms-Treaty Compliance.**

Department of Defense (Role in Arms Control). While the Senior Arms Control Review Group and the Arms Control and Disarmament Agency are the principal U.S. Government organizations responsible for arms control policy, several other executive agencies provide support for the formulation of policy. Of these, the Department of Defense plays the most significant role.

Support from the Department of Defense is principally on the military implications of arms control proposals and agreements, and the extent that they might alter the strategic balance between the United States and the Soviet Union. Because of the enormous size of the Department, and the complexity of the issues involved, the support/coordinating process is exceedingly slow, requiring inputs and reconciliation of views from numerous subordinate organizations (e.g. the Organization of the Joint Chiefs of Staff, the Unified and Specified Commands, the Services, the Defense Agencies, and others).

Disarmament. This is primarily a United Nations term which is used to characterize all measures relating to the prevention, limitation, and elimination of armaments and of military forces.

In the United States, the preferred term is "arms control." The United States Government, for instance, has no disarmament policy, as such, but it does have an arms control policy seeking the same ends as disarmament. Much of the confusion can probably be attributed to the fact that the basic U.S. law in this area (the Arms Control and Disarmament Act) uses both terms interchangeably.

Dual-capable Weapons. These are aircraft, missiles, and other weapons capable of handling either nuclear or nonnuclear munitions. Their increased use, especially in operational land- and sea-launched cruise missiles, is seriously complicating arms control verification problems. Short of a physical examination of their warheads, it is nearly impossible to determine whether cruise missiles are nuclear armed or not.

Effects of Nuclear War. Large-scale computer war games are conducted regularly by various agencies of the United States Government to develop assessments of the anticipated United States and Soviet losses from a general war. The latest such war games were conducted by the Arms Control and Disarmament Agency (ACDA) in April 1979.

Several attack scenarios were analyzed by ACDA, using the strategic balance as agreed upon under SALT II. The scenarios assumed a heavy Soviet first strike against U.S. strategic forces, military installations, and industry, followed by retaliatory strikes by U.S. forces against a similar set of Soviet targets. Civilian populations were not directly attacked. There were, nevertheless, high civilian fatalities on both sides, due to the proximity of civilian population concentrations to the military and industrial targets struck.

The ACDA concluded that, depending on the scenario used, human fatalities from the *short-term* effects of a nuclear general war would range from 25 to 100 million in each nation. Industrial damage, additionally, would range from 65 to 90% destruction of key production capacity. Urban devastation would be enormous, with over 200 cities in each country totally destroyed. *Long-term* effect would severely strain the economies, transportation networks, agriculture, and health conditions of both nations. Depending on fallout patterns, availability of food and water would be extremely critical; disease would be rampant; the millions of dead human and animal bodies would present enormous disposal problems; and major climatic and genetic changes would result.

Encryption of Telemetry. The encoding of telemetry for the purpose of rendering it undecipherable, and thus concealing the information recorded thereon, is known as encryption. The practice of encryption violates recent arms control agreements, most notably SALT I and II, which prohibit "deliberate concealment" whenever such activity is likely to impede verification.

Encoding of telemetry, as such, is not illegal under the terms of SALT I and II unless deliberate concealment (e.g. encryption) is involved. This very fine distinction has given rise to numerous charges and countercharges of noncompliance between the United States and the Soviet Union.

Environmental Modification Convention. The goal of this Convention is to prohibit the use of environmental modification techniques for military or hostile purposes. The term refers to any technique, which through the deliberate manipulation of natural processes, will cause a change in the dynamics, composition or structure of the earth, including its biota, lithosphere, hydrosphere, and atmosphere, or of the outer space.

The convention was signed in Geneva on May 18, 1977, culminating five years of intense United States–Soviet bilateral negotiations and concurrent deliberations within the then Committee on Disarmament. It entered into force on October 5, 1978. U.S. ratification was on December 13, 1979, after a unanimous vote in the Senate.

Under the terms of the convention, each signatory nation undertakes not to engage in military or other hostile use of environmental modification techniques having "widespread," "long-lasting," or "severe" effects, as a means of causing destruction, damage or injury to any other nation. "Widespread" is defined as encompassing an area on the scale of several hundred square kilometers; "long-lasting" is defined as lasting a period of months or approximately a season; "severe" is defined as involving serious or significant disruption or harm to human life, natural and economic resources or other assets. These commitments do not hinder, however, the use of environmental modification for peaceful purposes.

Escalation Control. Few arms control issues are of greater urgency than the need to develop processes which can control the scope of violence in a future military conflict involving the superpowers. The obvious goal is to prevent escalation from conventional to nuclear levels of combat, either by accident, miscalculation, or even deliberately.

Two requirements must be met if true escalation control is to be achieved: (1) Each side must have forces, so sized and equipped, as to be able to fight comfortably at the level selected by its enemy, without requiring to escalate to higher levels of violence. (2) A state of rough nuclear parity must prevail between the combatants, deterring each from electing the nuclear option. The absence of the first requirement, above, has necessitated the adoption by NATO of its present strategy, which calls for the use of tactical nuclear weapons to oppose a Soviet large-scale conventional attack in western Europe.

Executive Order 11850. This order, dated April 8, 1975, renounces as a matter of national policy the first use in war of chemical herbicides and of riot control agents. Exceptions include the use of chemical herbicides for control of vegetation within and around U.S. military bases and installations, and the use of riot control agents in defensive military modes designed to save lives. The Secretary of Defense is reponsible for ensuring that the United States armed forces do not use chemical herbicides or riot control agents in war, unless such use has prior Presidential approval.

Federal Emergency Management Agency (FEMA). This is the central planning and coordinating agency within the United States Government responsible for a wide range of emergency management activities, including the protection of the United States population and economy in the event of a nuclear accident or nuclear attack.

Since the ability to respond effectively to a major national emergency requires the support of government at all levels, FEMA carries out its responsibilities in close coordination with numerous other Federal, state, and local agencies. Protection of the nation's population from nuclear attack is, of course, a primary FEMA consideration and several civil defense programs have been promulgated by the agency with this goal in mind. Included are: the operation of warning systems, shelter planning and identification; plans for evacuating civilians in case of impending nuclear attack; and provision of emergency information through the Emergency Broadcast System.

The agency's total staff consists of approximately 2,500 personnel. The majority are assigned to ten regional offices. Two agency publications are noteworthy:
  - *In Time of Emergency—A Citizen's Handbook* (Chapter 10 deals with nuclear attack)
  - *What You Should Know About Nuclear Preparedness*

First Committee of the U.N. General Assembly. The Committee is the General Assembly's exclusive organ for dealing with disarmament and related international security questions. It consists of representatives of all member states and recommends relevant draft resolutions to the plenary membership of the Assembly for adoption. Decisions are made by a majority of the members present and voting.

During its 1983 session, the First Committee reviewed the progress made toward the implementation of the decisions of the First and Second Special Sessions on Disarmament of the U.N. General Assembly. Additionally, it considered issues relating to a nuclear test-ban treaty, the establishment of nuclear weapon-free zones, and the prevention of an arms race in outer space. See also **U.N. General Assembly.**

First Strike. This is the first offensive move in a nuclear war, carried out at such devastatingly high levels of violence, as to destroy an opponent's capability to launch a major counter-strike or to even continue in the conflict. Theoretically, a successful first strike will destroy not only the great majority of the victim's nuclear forces, but also his command and control facilities, population and economy. A first strike is by definition a preemptive action, launched by a nation when it believes that its national survival is at stake, or on the presumption that its adversary is about to launch a major nuclear attack.

A term frequently confused with first strike is "first use." The latter merely signifies the introduction of nuclear weapons at some stage of the conflict. One or more weapons could be involved.

First Use. See No First Use of Nuclear Weapons.

Five Continent Peace Initiative. On May 22, 1984, the presidents of Argentina, Mexico, and Tanzania, and the prime ministers of India, Sweden, and Greece, called on the nuclear-weapon states, particularly the United States and the Soviet Union, to reverse the nuclear arms race by halting the testing, production, and development of nuclear weapons and their delivery systems. Proclaiming that the prevention of a nuclear catastrophe is of the highest priority for mankind, the world leaders declared: "The people we represent are no less threatened by nuclear war than the citizens of the nuclear-weapons states."

The initiative received extensive and favorable media coverage worldwide, and support from numerous other government leaders. Encouraged by this development, the six world leaders plan to expand their activities for 1985. Early meetings are planned in New Delhi and Athens, as well as face-to-face discussions with the leaders of the nuclear powers to urge immediate adoption of a nuclear freeze and subsequent abolition of nuclear weapons.

French Nuclear Forces. The French nuclear forces are independent of NATO control. They consist of five ballistic submarines, equipped with 80 launchers, and 15 intermediate range missiles (IRBMS).

As in the case of the United Kingdom, France is planning a

major expansion of its nuclear forces. Major planned actions include the deployment of MIRVed missiles on its submarines, the use of air-to-surface missiles on its Mirage bombers, and the replacement of its single-warhead IRBMs with a multi-warhead mobile IRBM force.

Soviet concern over the increasing French nuclear capabilities became apparent during the Intermediate-Range Nuclear Forces (INF) negotiations in Geneva. The Soviet Union demanded that these forces be included in the agenda of the negotiations. The United States maintained, throughout, that the INF forum was "bilateral" (i.e. between the United States and the Soviet Union), and that therefore discussion of the French and British nuclear forces was inappropriate.

General Advisory Committee on Arms Control and Disarmament. This body was authorized by the Arms Control and Disarmament Act of 1961. Its purpose is to advise the President, the Secretary of State, and the Director of the Arms Control and Disarmament Agency on matters affecting arms control, disarmament, and world peace. The members of the Committee are appointed by the President with the advice and consent of the Senate. William R. Graham is the present Chairman.

Geneva Protocol. This is one of the oldest arms control agreements still in effect, having been signed in Geneva on June 17, 1925. A total of 127 nations have deposited instruments of ratification to the treaty or have declared themselves to be bound by its provisions. U.S. ratification was by President Ford on January 22, 1975. (The U.S. ratification, however, ceases to be binding for "chemical agents," should an enemy state or its allies fail to observe its provisions.)

The Convention prohibits the use in war of asphyxiating, poisonous or other gasses, and of bacteriological methods of warfare. It declares this prohibition to be "universally accepted as part of International Law, binding alike the conscience and practice of nations."

"Hot-Line" Agreement. The "Hot-Line" Agreement is the first bilateral arms control agreement signed between the United States and the Soviet Union. Although limited in scope at the time of its drafting, the agreement did give recognition to the grave perils implicit in modern nuclear weapons control. Signed in Geneva on June 20, 1963, it was subsequently "modernized" in 1971 and "upgraded" in 1984.

The Cuban missile crisis of October 1962 gave impetus to development of the agreement. The crisis proved the compelling need for prompt and direct communications between the heads of the governments of the United States and the Soviet Union, to reduce the danger that an accident, miscalculation, or surprise attack might trigger a nuclear war.

Under its terms, the United States and the Soviet Union agreed to establish a direct communications link between their governments. Each government is responsible for the link on its own territory, for ensuring the continuous functioning of the link, and for the prompt delivery to its head of government of any communications received by means of the link from the head of government of the other party. The direct communications link comprises:

- two terminal points with teletype equipment;
- a full-time duplex wire telegraph circuit (Washington-London-Copenhagen-Stockholm-Helsinki-Moscow); and,
- a full-time duplex radio telegraph circuit (Washington-Tangier-Moscow).

"Hot-Line" Modernization Agreement. This agreement, signed in Washington on September 30, 1971, was prompted by advances in satellite communications (since the original "Hot-Line" Agreement) and concern that the links, as constituted, may not survive or be reliable during a nuclear crisis. The resulting agreement provides for the establishment of two satellite communications circuits between the United States and the Soviet Union, supported by a system of multiple terminals in each country. The United States undertook to provide one circuit via the INTELSAT system and the Soviet Union via its MOLNIYA II system. Both circuits are now in place and operational.

"Hot-Line" Upgrade. The United States and the Soviet Union agreed on July 18, 1984 to upgrade the "Hot-Line" established under their agreement of June 20, 1963. The upgrade consists of the addition of high-speed facsimile equipment, which will permit the transmission between Moscow and Washington of graphic materials, such as maps, photos, and diagrams.

Indian Ocean as a Zone of Peace. In 1971, at the request of Sri Lanka, the United Nations General Assembly declared the Indian Ocean as a "Zone of Peace" and called upon all nations to withdraw from the area their military bases and installations, nuclear weapons, and other weapons of mass destruction. The task of translating the declaration into reality, by means of a "Conference on the Indian Ocean," was assigned to an Ad Hoc Committee.

To date, the Ad Hoc Committee has encountered stubborn

opposition in all its attempts to convene the Conference. Opposition has been especially strong on the part of France, the United States, the United Kingdom, and the Soviet Union, all concerned that their rights to free navigation might be jeopardized by the proposal. In a related development, the United States and the Soviet Union began bilateral talks in 1977 on the desirability of establishing military limitations in the Indian Ocean. These talks were suspended, however, in 1978 and have not been resumed since.

Inhumane Weapons Convention. This is the first international arms control agreement that has been negotiated at a United Nations conference. It provides rules for the protection of civilians and civilian property from certain weapons considered to be too cruel in their effects. These weapons include incendiary weapons, such as napalm; land mines and booby-traps; and weapon fragments that cannot be readily detected in the human body.

The initiative for convening a conference to prohibit or restrict the use of inhumane weapons originated in the United Nations General Assembly against the backdrop of the Vietnam War. On April 10, 1981, after three years of extended negotiations, the Convention was finally agreed upon and signature by forty nations followed. Thirteen additional states have signed since.

There are three Protocols attached to the basic Convention. Protocol I prohibits the use of fragments not detectable in the human body by means of X-rays. Protocol II imposes general restrictions on the use of mines, booby-traps, and other such devices. It also establishes rules for recording mines, minefields, and booby-traps, for ease of their removal after the cessation of hostilities. Protocol III prohibits the making of a civilian population the object of an incendiary attack, and otherwise restricts the use of incendiary weapons in a civilian environment.

Intermediate-Range Nuclear Forces (INF) Negotiations. The goal of these negotiations was the reduction of United States and Soviet intermediate-range nuclear forces stationed on the European continent. The negotiations were initiated in November 1981, but despite some apparent progress, were suspended by the Soviet Union on November 23, 1983, on deployment in Europe of the first Pershing II and Tomahawk missiles. Paul Nitze served as the United States representative to the INF negotiations. Yuli Kvitsinsky was his Soviet counterpart.

Principal impetus for the INF negotiations was the Soviet deployment in eastern Europe of the SS-20 weapons system. In 1979,

NATO reacted to this development by ordering the positioning in the United Kingdom, West Germany, Belgium, Netherlands, and Italy, of 108 Pershing II ballistic missiles and of 464 Tomahawk GLCMs (ground-launched cruise missiles). Simultaneously, NATO agreed to seek negotiations with the Soviet Union for the purpose of reaching an arms control agreement on the "most threatening systems on both sides."

Central Issues:

- The two sides were in disagreement on the specific forces to be considered in the negotiations. The United States stressed the need for controlling *land*-based missiles (e.g., the Soviet SS-20, SS-4, and SS-5 systems). The Soviets insisted on a consideration of all "medium" range systems, to include also U.S. dual-capable aircraft and the ballistic missiles in the British and French nuclear arsenals.

- The two sides disagreed also on the size and composition of the intermediate-range nuclear forces presently threatening the European continent. The United States maintained that the Soviet deployment of SS-20s, along with the older SS-4 and SS-5 ballistic systems, represented a total threat to Europe of some 1,200 warheads. The Soviet Union countered by arguing that there is a rough equivalence of forces in the "medium range." In making this claim, the Soviets included in their estimates the British and French nuclear forces as well as the U.S. dual-capable aircraft. (On the issue of the British and French national nuclear forces, the United States claimed lack of authority to negotiate. The INF forum, the United States argued, is "bilateral," i.e., between the United States and the Soviet Union, not "multilateral." Discussion of British and French national nuclear forces, therefore, would be inappropriate.)

- There was disagreement also on the geographic scope of the negotiations, the United States maintaining that the INF missile problem is *global*, as opposed to the Soviet *regional* view (i.e., European only). The issue has tremendous security inplications for the People's Republic of China and Japan. Both nations are concerned that the Soviet Union might decide to augment its already large INF advantage in Asia as a result of an agreement.

The United States position at the talks was embodied in President Reagan's speech of November 18, 1981. It proposed a cancellation of the planned U.S. deployment of the Pershing II and Tomahawk missiles, if the Soviet Union would agree to withdraw its

SS-20 system from the European continent. The President's proposal became known as the "zero/zero option," since its acceptance would have eliminated all medium-range, land-based nuclear systems from Europe.

In March 1983, when it became clear that the Soviets would not accept the "zero/zero option," the United States proposed an interim agreement. Under its terms, the United States would scale down its NATO deployment of Pershings and GLCMs, if the Soviets agreed to reduce their INF forces "to an equal level on a global basis." In September 1983, President Reagan announced three elaborations of this proposal, including a suggestion, two months later, for an equal ceiling of 420 INF warheads.

The initial Soviet proposal included two key points: a moratorium on further medium-range missile deployment for the duration of the negotiations; and a negotiated program of reductions of *all* medium-range weapons, including the British and French nuclear forces. As the negotiations progressed, the Soviets offered at least two alternate proposals. In each, they offered to reduce their SS-20 force in return for U.S. cancellation of the Pershing II and Tomahawk deployment plans.

International Atomic Energy Agency (IAEA). The IAEA is an autonomous institution within the United Nations system. Established in 1957, its mission is twofold: to assist member states (now numbering 118) in the development of their peaceful energy programs; and to apply safeguards to nuclear activities, worldwide, to ensure their peaceful intent. The agency's headquarters is in Vienna, Austria.

IAEA carries out its international safeguards activities by means of:

- on-site inspections of nuclear power reactors and of other nuclear facilities, to detect any possible diversion of nuclear material into components of a nuclear explosive;
- the maintenance of detailed accounts and records regarding the location, quantities, form and movement of nuclear materials;
- review of the design of nuclear facilities to ensure that provisions have been made for surveillance and other independent measuring devices.

All major nuclear suppliers now require IAEA safeguards on their exports. Some, including the United States, require recipient nations to have all their peaceful nuclear facilities under IAEA safeguards as a precondition.

Annually, IAEA conducts approximately 1,800 on-site inspections at 520 different locations. In its latest published report, the Agency reported no anomaly which would indicate the misuse of facilities or equipment, or the diversion of significant amounts of safeguarded material for unauthorized purposes.

Latin America Nuclear Free Zone Treaty. The Treaty for the Prohibition of Nuclear Weapons in Latin America was signed at Tlatelolco, a section of Mexico City, on February 14, 1967. It entered into force on April 22, 1968 and is currently in effect for 24 Latin American and Caribbean nations. The treaty seeks to limit the spread of nuclear weapons by preventing their introduction into areas hitherto free of them. Besides the basic agreement among the Latin American countries themselves, two additional protocols are provided as part of the accord: Protocol I which is applicable to non–Latin American countries that have possessions in the nuclear-free zone; and Protocol II which applies to powers (such as the United States) that already possess nuclear weapons.

Under the terms of the agreement, the contracting parties undertake to use exclusively for peaceful purposes the nuclear materials and facilities which are under their jurisdiction and pledge not to test, use, manufacture, or acquire nuclear weapons. These obligations are verified through the application of IAEA safeguards. Protocol I calls on the nations which have possessions in the nuclear-free zone to apply the denuclearization provisions of the treaty to their territories in the zone. Protocol II requires that nuclear-weapons states respect the denuclearized status of the zone and pledge not to use or threaten to use nuclear weapons against the contracting parties.

Limited Test Ban Treaty. The "Limited" Test Ban Treaty prohibits nuclear weapons tests or any other nuclear explosion in the atmosphere, in outer space, and under water. While not banning tests underground, the treaty does prohibit nuclear explosions in this environment also, if they are likely to cause radioactive debris to be present outside the territorial limits of the state under whose jurisdiction or control the explosions take place.

Efforts to achieve an "all-inclusive" test ban agreement began in the early 1950s and extended for almost a decade. They involved complex technical problems of verification and deep-seated United States and Soviet differences in approach to arms control and security. Negotiations finally culminated in a "limited" treaty, i.e. one which outlawed nuclear testing only in the environments where agreement could be reached. The treaty was signed in Moscow on August 5, 1963 and entered into force on October 10 of the same year. Throughout the period of negotiations, public interest was active and sustained, caused by the rising concern about the radioactive fallout resulting from U.S. and Soviet nuclear weapons tests. Apprehension was expressed by the scientific community on the possibility of a cumulative contamination of the environment and of resultant genetic damage.

Under the terms of the treaty, each party undertakes to prohibit, prevent, and refrain from conducting any nuclear weapon test or other nuclear explosion, at any place under its jurisdiction or control:

- in the atmosphere; beyond its limits, including outer space; or under water, including territorial waters or high seas; or
- in any other environment if such explosion would cause radioactive debris to be present outside the territorial limits of the state under whose jurisdiction or control such explosion is conducted.

Article III of the treaty opens it to all states, and most countries of the world have now signed it (111 nations are parties and an additional 15 nations have signed but not ratified). Of the nuclear-weapon states two holdouts remain: France and the People's Republic of China have declined thus far to sign the agreement.

Midgetman. A new, single-warhead ICBM, possibly a companion to or a substitute for the MX, being actively promoted by defense hawks and doves alike, and also strongly recommended by the President's Commission on Strategic Forces (Scowcroft Commission). The Midgetman will be light and fully mobile, and thus invulnerable to a Soviet nuclear attack. Deployment of about 1,000 missiles would be in the southwestern states during the 1990s.

Approximately $700 million are included in the DOD FY 1985 budget for Midgetman's research and development, including funds for alternative forms of basing (superhardened silos as well as mobile). Congress has mandated that key Midgetman subsystems be tested prior to January 1987, the deployment date for the first MX.

Monitoring. The term is used extensively in arms control documentation to describe the process of observing an opponent's activities, to ensure that he is complying with the provisions of applicable arms control agreements. Thus, the United States "monitors" Soviet compliance and the Soviets "monitor" the U.S., meaning that both nations are spying on each other by means of photo reconnaissance satellites and other technical intelligence collection systems. The purpose of these activities is to learn about the other's research and development programs, weapons testing, and other military activities, which might indicate a changed dimension in the threat or the strategic balance between the two nations.

Mutual and Balanced Force Reductions (MBFR). The MBFR negotiations aim at reducing the massive confrontation of conventional forces in Central Europe, specifically in the area covered by the territory of the Federal Republic of Germany, the German Democratic Republic, the Netherlands, Belgium, Luxembourg, Poland, and Czechoslovakia.

The negotiations were initiated in 1973 and are being held in Vienna, Austria. Participants are the twelve NATO allies and the seven Warsaw Pact countries.

Central Issues:

- There is disagreement on the size of the respective NATO/ Warsaw Pact ground forces in Central Europe. The United States claims that there is a disparity of ground forces (790,000 allied ground forces vs. 960,000 Warsaw Pact forces); the Warsaw Pact claims that a rough parity exists. In the United States view any agreement must be based on *agreed* manpower data.
- Geography gives the Soviet Union a significantly greater reinforcement capability in the area. At issue are the Soviet forces stationed in the western European U.S.S.R., but outside the territory provided in an eventual MBFR agreement.
- NATO insists on a program of confidence-building and verification measures, including inspection, to complement the actual reductions in an eventual agreement.

The NATO position is embodied in a draft treaty presented to the Warsaw Pact nations on July 8, 1982. It provides for legally binding commitments by all participants to reduce force levels within seven years—to approximately 900,000 ground and air forces on each side, no more than 700,000 of which to be ground forces. Reductions are to be taken in four stages and be based on agreed manpower data. Associated confidence-building and verification measures are included in the draft treaty.

The Warsaw Pact position is embodied in a draft agreement tabled in February 1982. It provides for United States and Soviet reductions in an *initial* reduction phase (postponing discussion of later actions). The draft agreement proposes modest confidence-building measures but does not address the issue of manpower data.

In February 1983, the Warsaw Pact made a further proposal, the principal elements of which are:

- U.S./Soviet reductions to be by "mutual example," i.e., to be made outside the context of an agreement.

- An agreed freeze on all forces and armaments in the MBFR area, subsequent to the U.S./Soviet withdrawals;
- Subsequent negotiation of a binding treaty to be based on the Warsaw Pact proposal of February 1982.

Mutual Assured Destruction. This is the current U.S. strategy of deterrence. It is based on the realization that both the United States and the Soviet Union possess the ability to inflict an "unacceptable degree of damage" on each other by means of a second strike, after absorbing a first strike. The purpose of U.S. nuclear forces, therefore, is to deter the Soviets from using theirs.

A "second strike" is the ability of a nation to survive a nuclear attack and to launch a retaliatory blow large enough to inflict intolerable damage to the opponent. "Unacceptable damage" is the destruction anticipated from a second strike, which is sufficient to deter a nuclear power from launching a first strike.

MX. The MX weapon system, officially the "Peacekeeper," is an intercontinental ballistic missile presently under development. Extraordinarily lethal (its 10 warheads together are 350 times more destructive than the Hiroshima bomb), it is expected to become the most accurate and reliable land-based ICBM in the nuclear arsenal of either superpower. As currently planned, 100 MXs will be deployed beginning in January 1987. The Government estimates the cost of the program at $16.6 billion, expressed in 1982 dollars. Others estimate the cost at $21 billion.

Research and development of the MX began more than a decade ago. Full-scale development, however, was not authorized until September 1979. President Carter, who took the action, favored a program level of 200 missiles deployed for survivability in a "race-track" pattern of 4,600 shelters. The plan was scrapped, however, by President Reagan in favor of 100 MX missiles deployed in closely-spaced superhardened silos (the "dense pack"). When the Congress balked at this plan too, the President sought assistance from a Commission on Strategic Forces (the Scowcroft Commission). Its recommendation for deploying the MX in existing missile silos in Nebraska and Wyoming represents current official policy.

Development and production of the MX is generally on schedule, despite numerous efforts in the Congress to limit the number of missiles to be built or even to kill the program outright. Through the years, various production levels have been discussed. As of this writing, the Congress has appropriated funds for the production and deployment of 42 missiles only. Future plans are uncertain. For FY 1986 the Administration has requested funds for 48 additional missiles, but there is much opposition within both houses of Congress, especially on the basing plans for the MX. Closely related to this issue is the potential use of the MX as a "bargaining chip" in U.S.–Soviet arms control negotiations underway in spring 1985 between the United States and the Soviet Union.

Supporters of the MX claim that the system restores U.S.–Soviet parity in land-based ICBM systems, thus enhancing international stability through improved deterrence. Critics refer to the missile as a "fatal mistake" and characterize it as a dangerous first strike weapon, especially when viewed along with the other weapons in the U.S. strategic forces modernization program (e.g. the B-1B bomber, the Stealth bomber, the Midgetman, the Pershing II, the cruise missiles, and the Trident D 5).

National Technical Means (NTM). This is the name for the intelligence collection systems which are used by the superpowers to monitor compliance with the provisions of an arms control agreement. The better known NTM include photo-reconnaissance satellites, aircraft- and ship-based systems (such as radars and antennas used for collecting telemetry), and large ground stations which monitor missile tests and aircraft flights.

The NTM are the offically designated means of verification in SALT I and II and in several other international arms control accords negotiated under U.N. auspices. They provide the opportunity to verify compliance with treaty provisions without requiring access to the territory of the other nation. Provisions in the SALT agreements, which are designed to strengthen the role of the NTM, include commitments not to interfere with their operation and to abstain from deliberate concealment designed to impede verification.

NATO "Dual-Track" Decision. The Intermediate-Range Nuclear Force negotiations between the United States and the Soviet Union, which began in Geneva in November 1981, resulted from the 1979 NATO decision on "force modernization and arms control" (the "Dual-Track" decision), the purpose of which was to redress the strategic imbalance on the European continent caused by the massive Soviet build-up of SS-20s beginning in 1977.

The decision, adopted unanimously by the NATO foreign ministers on December 12, 1979, proposed that immediate negotiations be held between the United States and the Soviet Union, for the purpose of redressing the SS-20 deployment. The decision also stipulated that, in the absence of an agreement, NATO would deploy 572 intermediate-range missiles in five countries: United Kingdom, Federal Republic of Germany, Italy, Belgium, and the Netherlands. The missiles to be deployed were 108 Pershing IIs and 464 Ground-launched Cruise Missiles (GLCMs). On November 23, 1983, on deployment in Western Europe of the first Pershing IIs and the Tomahawk GLCMs, the Soviet Union walked out of the Geneva-based INF and START negotiations.

As of January 1985, deployment of the Pershing II and Tomahawk GLCMs is on schedule. However, political problems have caused the government of the Netherlands to postpone a decision on cruise missile deployment until November 1985.

Negative Security Assurances. The purpose of this initiative is to develop legally binding international arrangements which would provide assurances to non–nuclear-weapons states that nuclear weapons would not be used against them. The issue is being debated extensively within the Conference on Disarmament and the United Nations General Assembly.

Several nonnuclear states are behind this effort. In their view, the nuclear-weapons states are under obligation to guarantee in clear and categorical terms that the non–nuclear-weapons states will not become victims of threat or attack with nuclear weapons. They criticize the "no-first-use" pledges of the nuclear-weapons states as being vague, "qualified," and full of loopholes.

Of the nuclear-weapons states, only the People's Republic of China has come out with an unconditional pledge not to use or threaten to use such weapons against non–nuclear-weapons countries and nuclear-free zones. The French and United Kingdom positions are very similar to that of the United States. In effect, they pledge not to use nuclear weapons against any non–nuclear-weapons state which is party to the Non-Proliferation Treaty, except in the case of attack on their territory or the territory of their allies. The Soviet pledge is worded differently. It declares that it will never use nuclear weapons against those states which renounce the production and acquisition of such weapons and do not have them on their territories.

No First Use of Nuclear Weapons. This is a grass-roots initiative (enjoying also broad support in NATO Europe) growing out of public concern that the United States Government has never officially renounced the "first use" of nuclear weapons. In contrast, both the Soviet Union and the People's Republic of China have repeatedly declared their commitment not to be "first users" of nuclear weapons.

The No First Use proposal would make it a matter of policy for the United States not to be the first nation to use nuclear weapons in the event of military conflict. Conventional forces (rather than nuclear) would be relied upon to defend U.S. security and interests, with nuclear forces being maintained only as a deterrent to the hostile use of nuclear forces. The policy would serve as an alternative to current NATO strategy which calls for the use of nuclear weapons by the alliance to turn back a conventional Soviet attack against Western Europe.

Proponents of the No First Use policy maintain that the use of nuclear weapons can never really remain "limited." Even the detonation of one nuclear weapon will ultimately lead to an all-out escalation and a nuclear holocaust. No First Use, if adopted and accompanied by improvements in NATO's conventional defenses, will reduce U.S. and NATO reliance on nuclear weapons, diminish the risk of nuclear war, and strengthen the credibility of the Western deterrent to Soviet aggression. Opponents of the policy argue that a No First Use pledge will nullify the value of nuclear weapons as instruments of deterrence.

Non-Proliferation Treaty. The "Treaty on the Non-Proliferation of Nuclear Weapons" is the fundamental instrument of international nonproliferation policy. It was signed in Washington, London, and Moscow on July 1, 1968 and entered into force on March 5, 1970. A total of 122 nations are party to the agreement.

According to its provisions, nuclear-weapons states undertake not to transfer nuclear weapons or other nuclear explosive devices to any recipient, and non–nuclear-weapons states undertake not to receive the transfer of nuclear weapons or other nuclear explosive devices, nor to manufacture them or otherwise acquire them. The treaty does not impinge on the right of nations to employ nuclear energy for peaceful purposes, with the potential benefits of peaceful application of nuclear explosion technology being made available to nonnuclear parties. A provision in the treaty calls for periodic conferences to review operations with a view to assuring that its basic purposes are being met. Two such Review Conferences have been held thus far (in 1975 and 1980). The 3rd Review Conference is scheduled to be held in Geneva during 1985.

The Non-Proliferation Treaty has often been termed an "unequal treaty," because it imposes heavier obligations on the non–nuclear-weapons states than on the nuclear-weapons states. All parties to the treaty, however, undertake in Article VI "to pursue negotiations in good faith on effective measures relating to cessation of the nuclear arms race at an early date and to nuclear disarmament, and on a treaty on general and complete disarmament under strict and effective international control."

Nuclear Freeze Campaign. The Nuclear Weapons Freeze Campaign had its beginning late in 1979, when a draft paper entitled "The Call to Halt the Nuclear Arms Race" was circulated to a number of well-known arms control experts, directors of national organizations, and peace groups around the country. The paper called upon the leaders of the United States and the Soviet Union to stop the nuclear arms race, specifically to "adopt a mutual freeze on the testing, production, and deployment of nuclear weapons and of missiles and new aircraft designed primarily to deliver nuclear weapons."

Since March 1981, when the national campaign was begun, support for the freeze has broadened and deepened. Hundreds of city councils, county bodies and town meetings have endorsed the freeze, including one or both houses of the legislatures in 23 states. Additionally, 60 state and local freeze referendums have been held across the nation. Overall, 60% of those voting have favored the freeze.

Supporters of the nuclear freeze concept argue that:
- the greatest challenge facing mankind is to prevent the occurrence of a nuclear war, by accident or by design;
- the nuclear arms race is dangerously increasing the risk of a holocaust (humanity's last act);
- the proposed freeze is a logical and practical way to curb the arms race and reduce the threat of a nuclear war.

Opponents argue that:
- the freeze would sanction present nuclear weaponry levels, which are unacceptably high on both sides;
- it would undermine NATO's December 1979 "Dual Track" decision on intermediate nuclear forces and the alliance's efforts to negotiate the total elimination of all nuclear land-based missiles in Europe;
- it would be enormously difficult to verify;
- it would lock in forever the strategic superiority presently enjoyed by the Soviet Union.

In response to public demand on this issue, several members of the Congress have introduced legislation favoring adoption of a nuclear freeze. All such efforts have been defeated in the Senate. However, a resolution favoring an "immediate, mutual, and verifiable freeze" was approved in the House of Representatives on May 4, 1983 by a vote of 278–149.

Nuclear Material Convention. The "Convention on the Physical Protection of Nuclear Material" resulted from concern that the "unlawful taking and use" of nuclear material might pose grave dangers to mankind. The convention was adopted in Vienna on October 26, 1979, but was not opened to signature until March 3, 1980. Thirty-seven states, including the United States, are signatories. A total of twenty nations must deposit instruments of ratification before the convention will enter force.

The parties to the convention undertake to take appropriate steps to protect nuclear material within their territory, during international transport, or while onboard a ship or aircraft under their jurisdiction. They also agree to recover and return any nuclear material stolen while in international shipment.

Nuclear Nonproliferation. Nuclear proliferation poses a serious threat to international peace and stability and to the security interests of all nations. Accordingly, a fundamental objective of the international community is to prevent the spread of nuclear weapons to additional countries. Accords which attempt to control nuclear proliferation include the Treaty on the Non-Proliferation of Nuclear Weapons (signed July 1, 1968) and the Treaty for the Prohibition of Nuclear Weapons in Latin America (signed February 14, 1967).

Despite continuing international efforts to prevent further proliferation, additional nations may soon be acquiring nuclear weapons. Proliferation will further increase the potential for nuclear conflict, especially in the following four regions of high tension:

South Asia: India has demonstrated a nuclear capability, but has refrained from further nuclear testing since its initial underground test in 1974. India, however, is not party to the Non-Proliferation Treaty and its nuclear facilities are not subject to IAEA safeguards. Pakistan, India's rival, is constructing nuclear facilities, including a uranium enrichment plant, which could produce fissile material. India has resisted all efforts to bring its nuclear facilities under international safeguards and has refused to rule out the "nuclear option."

Middle East: Proliferation potential in this area is extremely high. Israel's nuclear program, the most advanced in the region, is still without international safeguards. Libya has an embryonic nuclear program but hopes to acquire a nuclear capability. Iraq's nuclear reactor was destroyed by an Israeli raid. Efforts to rebuild have been frustrated by the Iran-Iraqi war.

South Africa: South Africa has a very advanced nuclear program. The nation has not committed itself, as yet, to either the Non-Proliferation Treaty or the IAEA safeguards.

Latin America: Argentina has the region's most advanced nuclear program. Its government has confirmed the existence in country of a plant for enriching uranium, and although pledging itself to "exclusively peaceful means," it has rejected all international safeguards or accession to the Non-Proliferation Treaty. Brazil, the second Latin nation with a nuclear potential, has the technical know-how but not the resources to pursue the development of nuclear weapons.

Nuclear Non-Proliferation Act. The purpose of this Act (signed into law on March 10, 1978) is to provide for more efficient and effective control over the proliferation of nuclear explosive capability. In it, the Congress declares that the proliferation of nuclear explosive devices, or of the capability to manufacture or acquire such devices, "poses a grave threat to the security interests of the United States and to continued international progress toward world peace...."

The Act confirms national policy on a number of critical nonproliferation issues:

- It confirms continued United States support for the principles of the Treaty on the Non-Proliferation of Nuclear Weapons.
- It assures nations that seek to utilize the benefits of atomic energy for peaceful purposes, that the United States will provide a reliable supply of nuclear fuel (subject to their adherence to policies designed to prevent proliferatiion).
- It pledges to cooperate with other nations in establishing programs to assist them in the development of nonnuclear energy resources, and in aiding developing countries to meet their energy needs.

Nuclear Weapon Free Zones. The international community has given increased attention during the past years to the establishment of "nuclear weapon free zones" as a means of halting the spread of nuclear weapons. Such zones presently exist in Latin America, the Antarctica, on the seabed, and in outer space. Specific geographic areas which have been proposed for designation as nuclear weapon free, include: Central Europe; the Middle East; Africa; the Balkans; the Baltic and Scandinavian regions; and others.

An area to be designated as a "nuclear weapon free zone" must agree to refrain from producing, acquiring, or possessing nuclear weapons, and from introducing nuclear weapons into the area and/or using them against another state within the free zone. An international system of verification and control must exist to ensure and guarantee compliance.

Supporters of free zones maintain that their establishment will greatly enhance international peace and security by providing a powerful instrument to supplement the Treaty on the Non-Proliferation of Nuclear Weapons. Opponents claim that free zone proposals are mere ploys on the part of certain nations whose security interests require such designations.

Nuclear Weapons Effects. When a nuclear bomb or missile explodes, the main effects produced are intense light (flash), heat, blast, and radiation. The strength of these effects depends on the size and type of the weapon; the distance from the explosion; the prevailing weather conditions (sunny or rainy, windy or still); the terrain (whether flat or hilly); and the height of burst (high up in the air or near the earth's surface).

What effect a nuclear explosion is likely to have on one, depends on his/her nearness to the nuclear fireball. Generally, persons near a nuclear explosion would be killed instantly or become seriously injured by the blast, heat or initial nuclear radiation. Those several miles away would be endangered by the blast and heat and/or by the fires that the explosion might start. People surviving these hazards would still be endangered by radioactive fallout.

When a nuclear weapon explodes near the ground, great quantities of pulverized earth and other debris are sucked up into the nuclear cloud. There, the radioactive gases produced by the explosion condense on and into this debris, producing radioactive fallout particles. (Fallout particles may range in size from those resembling grains of sand to very small units that appear as fine dust). Within 15 to 30 minutes, the particles fall back to earth—the larger ones first, the smaller later. On their way down, and after they reach the ground, the radioactive particles give off invisible gamma rays like X-rays. Danger to humans is greatest during the first 24 hours of fall.

Nuclear Winter. Theory advanced by astronomer Carl Sagan and other scientists to the effect that a large-scale thermonuclear exchange between the superpowers would result in the earth's being encircled by a dense pall of smoke. The smoke, rising from the burning cities, would prevent the sun's rays from warming the earth thus resulting in a dark and frigid condition on earth which could possibly end all mankind. Nuclear winter, probably lasting for several months, would prevent crops from growing (thus resulting in widespread starvation), fresh water supplies would freeze, and various forms of life would gradually be eliminated. The nuclear winter theory is not disputed by knowledgeable military persons.

On-Site Inspection. This is a method of arms control verification (strongly supported by the United States, but opposed by the Soviet Union) whereby representatives of an international organization or the parties to an agreement, are allowed access to each other's territory to view force deployments and weapons systems. No arms accord has been negotiated as yet which embodies these procedures, except possibly for the "Treaty on Underground Nuclear Explosions for Peaceful Purposes" (not ratified by the United States Senate as of this writing).

The issue of on-site inspection probably accounts more than any other for the lack of progress in two critical arms control areas: nuclear testing and chemical weapons control. In the case of the former, the United States has requested (and the Soviets refused) up to seven inspections annually of small underground nuclear test sites in the Soviet Union. For chemical weapons control, the United States on-site inspection demands are even harsher. The United States is in effect demanding "anytime," "anywhere" access, as essential for assurance in the effective verification of compliance.

Soviet opposition to on-site inspection has traditionally been attributed to fears that the process is merely a United States ploy for conducting intelligence operations within the Soviet Union. During the past few years, however, the Soviets appear to be softening their opposition, even expressing willingness to discuss a concept of their making, i.e. "inspections by challenge".

Outer Space Treaty. The "Treaty on Outer Space and Celestial Bodies" was the second of the so-called post-World War II "nonarmament" treaties, its concept and some of its provisions being modeled after the Antarctic Treaty. It resulted from pledges, before the United Nations General Assembly, on the part of the United States and the Soviet Union, not to orbit weapons of mass destruction, install them on celestial bodies or station them in outer space. As finally negotiated, the treaty was opened for signature in Washington, London, and Moscow on January 27, 1967 and entered into force on October 10 of the same year. Although the treaty lacked verification provisions, the Senate gave it its unanimous consent, resting on the capabilities of the United States tracking network to detect any illegal launchings or devices in orbit. Eighty-nine other nations have signed and ratified.

Key treaty provisions are in Article IV which commit the parties to the agreement: not to undertake to place in orbit around the Earth any object carrying nuclear weapons or other weapons of mass destruction; not to install such weapons on celestial bodies or to station such weapons in outer space in any other manner. Additionally, Article IV provides that the moon and other celestial bodies shall be used by all states exclusively for peaceful purposes. The establishment of military bases, installations and fortifications, the testing of any type of weapons, and the conduct of military maneuvers on celestial bodies are strictly forbidden.

Pastoral Letter on War and Peace. The letter, issued on May 3, 1983 by the National Conference of Catholic Bishops, defines the position of the Catholic Church on a whole range of nuclear issues. Although addressing itself to the Catholic community in the United States, the Letter attempts to make a contribution also to the public debate, worldwide, on the dangers and dilemmas of the nuclear age.

The Letter describes the arms race as "one of the greatest curses on the human race" and as a "folly which does not provide the security it promises." It urges negotiations to cease the arms race and to ban nuclear weapons. As for nuclear weapons use, the Letter affirms the Bishops' view that "under no circumstances may nuclear weapons or other instruments of mass slaughter be used for the purpose of destroying populated centers or other predominantly civilian targets." The Bishops, the Letter adds, "do not perceive any situation in which deliberate initiation of nuclear war...can be morally justified" and they urge "NATO to move rapidly toward the adoption of a "no first use" policy."

Pershing II. This is the United States intermediate-range missile presently being deployed in western Europe. Its appearance on the European continent in November 1983, along with the first Tomahawk cruise missiles, resulted in the Soviet walk-out from the Intermediate-Range Nuclear Forces negotiations in Geneva.

The Pershing II is a much more accurate weapon system than its Soviet counterpart (the SS-20). It does not require a pre-surveyed launch position and can be reloaded and fired at a very fast rate. Although a tactical weapon, its range is about 1,800 km (2,500 km according to the Soviets), thus being able to reach within a few minutes of launch numerous targets in the European Soviet Union. A total of 108 Pershing IIs are planned for deployment in the Federal Republic of Germany under NATO's "Dual Track" decision of December 1979. At least half of these missiles are already in place.

Poseidon. The term is applied to both submarine-launched ballistic missiles and the submarines which launch them. At present the U.S. has 31 Poseidon submarines (each with 16 ballistic missile launchers), only 19 of which carry Poseidon (C-3) missiles; 12 are equipped with Trident I (C-4) missiles. During the 1990s, the entire Poseidon force is expected to be replaced by Trident submarines.

Prevention of Nuclear War Agreement. In this agreement, signed in Washington on June 22, 1973, the United States and the Soviet Union agreed to bring about world conditions which would reduce the danger of an outbreak of nuclear war and ultimately eliminate it. The agreement, an outgrowth of the state visit to the U.S. of Communist Party Chief Brezhnev, is of unlimited duration.

Under the terms of the agreement, the two parties pledged:

- to act in such a manner as to prevent the development of dangerous situations, to avoid military confrontations, and to exclude the outbreak of nuclear war between themselves and other countries;
- not to threaten or use force against each other or other countries in situations which may endanger international peace and security;
- to be guided by these considerations when formulating their foreign policies and in their actions in the field of international relations; and
- to enter into urgent consultations, whenever relations between them appear to involve the risk of nuclear war.

Radiological Weapons Control. The development of an international treaty prohibiting the development, production, stockpiling and use of radiological weapons is being pursued by the Conference on Disarmament with active support from the United States and the Soviet Union. Related to this effort are deliberations on the subject of prohibiting attacks against nuclear facilities, since in effect such attacks would be tantamount to the use of radiological weapons.

Although considerable differences remain, a draft "Treaty Prohibiting Radiological Weapons" was developed in 1983. Three principal issues still impede final approval of the draft treaty: the definition of "radiological weapons;" questions of compliance and verification; and the need for an appropriate provision for peaceful uses of radiological materials.

Safeguards. Nuclear safeguards as applied by the IAEA are the means for verifying that the nuclear activities of nations are consistent with their international commitments. Most of these commitments flow from the Treaty on the Non-Proliferation of Nuclear Weapons. A corollary objective of safeguards is to provide assurance to the international community that the various nations are complying with their non proliferation and "other peaceful use" undertakings, and that any possible diversion of nuclear material for military purposes can be properly detected.

Safeguards are applied by requiring operators of nuclear plants to keep accurate records of the movement of nuclear material in and out of plants, as well as during plant processes. These records are subject to IAEA verification by regular visits to plant facilities. Increasingly, use is being made of safeguard instruments, which are capable of recording movements of nuclear material between inspections. The IAEA is also making use of tamper-proof seals to secure stores of nuclear material between inspections and/or to seal the cores of the reactors themselves.

SALT I (Strategic Arms Limitation Talks). Negotiations leading to the SALT I agreements extended over a period of twelve years. When finally concluded in May 1972, they provided for two instruments: a "Treaty on the Limitation of Anti-Ballistic Missile Systems" (the ABM Treaty) and an "Interim Agreement on Certain Measures with Respect to the Limitation of Strategic Offensive Arms" (the Interim Agreement). In the ABM Treaty, the United States and the Soviet Union moved to end the competition in defensive systems that had threatened to spur offensive competition to still greater heights. In the Interim Agreement, the two nations took the first step to check the rivalry in their most powerful land- and submarine-based nuclear weapons.

The two accords differ in their duration and inclusiveness. The ABM Treaty is of unlimited duration, but each party has the right to withdraw on six months' notice if it decides that its supreme interests are jeopardized by "extraordinary events related to the subject matter of the Treaty." The Interim Agreement was for a five-year span and covered only certain major aspects of strategic weaponry. The two accords were accompanied by a number of "Agreed Statements," "Common Understandings," and "Unilateral Statements."

Both the ABM Treaty and the Interim Agreement stipulate that compliance is to be assured by "national technical means of verification," with both nations undertaking not to interfere with their operation. In addition, the signatory nations agreed not to use deliberate concealment measures to impede verification. The accords were signed in Moscow on May 26, 1972 and entered into force October 3, 1972.

SALT I ABM Treaty. Negotiations of the ABM Treaty proceeded from the premise that effective measures to limit anti-ballistic missile systems would be a substantial factor in curbing the arms race and thus decreasing the risk of nuclear war.

The United States and the Soviet Union agreed to allow each other two ABM deployment areas (this was subsequently reduced to only one area – refer to entry SALT I ABM Protocol). These areas were to be located and restricted so as to preclude the development and internetting of a nationwide ABM defense system. Each side may have one "limited" ABM site to protect its capital city and another to defend an ICBM launch area, provided that the two sites are at least 1,300 km apart.

At each site there may be no more than 100 interceptor missiles and 100 launchers. Additionally, both parties agreed to limit improvements in their ABM technology and to bar the utilization of interceptor missiles with more than one independently guided warhead. Deployment of radars intended to give early warning of strategic ballistic missile attack was not prohibited in the Treaty, but all such facilities were required to be located along the territorial boundaries of each country and be oriented outward (so as to preclude an ABM defense of the interior).

The Treaty provides for two mechanisms to promote its objectives and implementation. The first is the establishment of a U.S.-Soviet Standing Consultative Commission to consider questions of compliance and for reconciling any misunderstandings or uncertainties arising under treaty obligations. The second is a provision for treaty reviews at five-year intervals. (These reviews have been held on a regular basis since 1972, concluding that the ABM Treaty adequately serves the national interests of both nations.)

SALT I ABM Protocol. The SALT I ABM Treaty had permitted each side two ABM deployment areas, one to defend its national capital, the second to protect an ICBM launch site. The ABM Protocol, signed in Moscow on July 3, 1974, limits each side to one ABM deployment area only.

Under its terms, each party is allowed one ABM deployment area, but may change its site selection. Such a change, however, may be made once and only after advance notice to the other party. The Protocol is considered part of the 1972 SALT I ABM Treaty and its verification and other provisions continue to apply.

The Soviet Union has chosen to maintain its ABM defense of Moscow while the United States chose to defend its ICBM emplacements near Grand Forks, North Dakota. The United States area, however, has actually been on inactive status since 1976.

SALT I Interim Agreement. This is an "interim" agreement between the United States and the Soviet Union pending negotiation and conclusion of a more comprehensive accord for the limitation of strategic offensive arms. Many of its provisions parallel those in the SALT I ABM Treaty, and as with the latter, verification for compliance is assigned to "national technical means."

The agreement has essentially two main provisions:

- it freezes at existing levels the number of fixed, land-based ICBMs, operational and under construction, on each side, as of July 1, 1972;
- it limits submarine-launched ballistic missile launchers (SLBMs) and modern missile submarines, as follows:
    - U.S.: 710 SLBMs and no more than 44 modern ballistic missile submarines.
    - U.S.S.R.: 950 SLBMs and no more than 62 modern ballistic missile submarines.

Since neither side is allowed to begin construction of additional fixed, land-based ICBMs, the agreement in effect bars also the relocation of existing launchers. Additionally, the agreement prohibits the conversion into modern heavy ICBMs of launchers of light or older origin. However, within these limitations, modernization and replacement are permitted. There is no provision in the agreement concerning mobile ICBMs.

The provisions of the SALT I ABM Treaty for a U.S.-Soviet standing Consultative Commission are repeated in the Interim Agreement.

SALT II. In the SALT I Interim Agreement, the United States and the Soviet Union agreed to continue active negotiations to bring about further limitations in strategic offensive arms. The goal of the SALT II negotiations, therefore, was to replace the Interim Agreement with a long-term comprehensive treaty providing specific limitations in strategic offensive weapons systems.

The SALT II negotiations, launched in November 1972, stalled repeatedly over several issues. A breakthrough occurred at the Vladivostok summit (in November 1974), when President Ford and Communist Party Chief Brezhnev agreed on the following basic framework for the SALT agreement:

- an aggregate limit of 2,400 strategic nuclear delivery vehicles (ICBMs, SLBMs, and heavy bombers) on each side;
- an aggregate limit of 1,320 MIRV systems, each side;
- a ban on the construction of new land-based ICBM launchers;
- limits on the deployment of new types of strategic offensive arms; and,

- important elements of the Interim Agreement (such as those relating to verification) to be incorporated in the new agreement.

Despite the Vladivostok agreement, fundamental differences between the two sides persisted. (Examples: How should cruise missiles be addressed? Is the "Backfire" a "heavy bomber"?) With the advent of the Carter Administration, a further issue was added: the United States now favored significant reductions and qualitative constraints to the ceilings agreed upon at Vladivostok. In subsequent negotiations, a compromise agreement was worked out which accommodated both the Soviet desire to retain the Vladivostok framework and the United States proposal for more comprehensive limitations.

As signed in Vienna, on June 18, 1979, the SALT II agreement consists of three parts:

- a Treaty (effective until the end of 1985)
- a Protocol (of three years duration)
- a Joint Statement of Principles.

President Carter transmitted the SALT II agreement to the Senate for its advice and consent on June 22, 1979. Senate debate was interrupted, however, by the Soviet invasion of Afghanistan, an event which greatly affected the U.S.–Soviet relations. On January 3, 1980, President Carter asked the Senate to withdraw SALT II from debate and consideration. The Senate complied.

The talks have been set aside by the Reagan Administration and a new offensive arms agreement is being pursued through the Strategic Arms Reduction Talks (START). In the interim, both the United States and the Soviet Union have pledged not to take any action which would jeopardize the SALT II treaty, as long as the other side abides by its provisions.

Key Provisions:

(a) *Treaty*:

- an equal aggregate limit on the number of strategic nuclear delivery vehicles (ICBM and SLBM launchers, heavy bombers, and air-to-surface ballistic missiles [ASBMs]). Initially, the ceiling would be 2,400, as agreed at Vladivostok; the ceiling would be lowered by the end of 1981 to 2,250;
- an equal aggregate of 1,320 on the total number of launchers of MIRVed ballistic missiles and heavy bombers with long-range cruise missiles;
- an equal aggregate limit of 1,200 on the total number of launchers of MIRVed ballistic missiles; and,
- an equal aggregate limit of 820 on launchers of MIRVed ICBMs.

In addition of the above limits, the treaty provides for:

- a ban on the construction of additional fixed ICBM launchers and on increases in the number of fixed heavy ICBM launchers;
- a ban on heavy mobile ICBM launchers and on launchers of heavy SLBMs and ASBMs;
- a ban on flight-testing or deployment of new types of ICBMs, with the exception of one new type of light ICBM on each side;
- a ban on increasing the numbers of warheads on existing types of ICBMs, and a limit of 10 warheads on the one new type of ICBM permitted to each side;
- ceilings on the launch weight and throw weight of strategic ballistic missiles and a ban on the conversion of light ICBM launchers to launchers of heavy ICBMs;
- a ban on the Soviet SS-16 ICBM;
- a ban on rapid reload ICBM systems;
- a ban on certain new types of strategic offensive systems which, although technologically feasible, have not been deployed as yet; and,
- advance notification of certain ICBM test launches.

Treaty verification is by National Technical Means, including the use of photo-reconnaissance satellites, with both sides agreeing not to interfere (through concealment or countermeasures) with each others' verification activities.

(b) *Protocol*:

- a ban on the deployment of mobile ICBM launchers and the flight testing of ICBMs from such launchers;
- a ban on the deployment of cruise missiles of ranges in excess of 600 kilometers on ground- and sea-based launchers; and,
- a ban on flight testing and deployment of air-to-surface ballistic missiles (ASBMs).

Further negotiations on these issues were deferred to SALT III.

(c) *Joint Statement of Principles*:

- the parties agreed to continue to pursue negotiations on measures for the further limitation and reduction in the numbers of strategic arms, as well as for their further qualitative limitations;
- further limitations and reductions must be subject to adequate verification by National Technical Means;
- the United States and Soviet Union agreed to consider other steps to enhance strategic stability, mutual equality and security.

Scowcroft Commission. In January 1983, President Reagan established a "Special Commission on Strategic Forces" to review the United States strategic forces program, particularly the future of land-based ICBMs, and to provide recommendations for greater stability. The commission, popularly known as the Scowcroft Commission after its chairman, retired General Brent Scowcroft, delivered its report to the President on April 6, 1983.

The Scowcroft Commission recommended:

- Continued improvements in U.S. command, control and communications, and continuation of U.S. bomber, submarine, and cruise missile programs.
- Modernization of U.S. ICBM forces, including the deployment of 100 new MX missiles, and initiation of developmental work on a small, single-warhead ICBM.
- A major research effort in strategic defense and on ways to increase the survivability of U.S. land-based forces.

The President endorsed the Scowcroft Commission's recommendations and ordered that they be incorporated into the START negotiating position.

Seabed Arms Control Treaty. The Seabed Treaty seeks to prevent the introduction of international conflict and nuclear weapons into an area hitherto free of them. In this respect, it resembles the Antarctic Treaty, the Outer Space Treaty, and the Latin American Nuclear-Free Zone Treaty.

Impetus for the Seabed Arms Control Treaty came from advances in the technology of oceanography, and concern that the vast and virtually untapped resources of the ocean floor might lead to strife. Additionally, there were fears that nations might use the seabed as a new environment for military installations, including those capable of launching nuclear weapons.

Negotiations leading toward the treaty were held in various U.N. forums beginning in August 1967 and extended for over two years. Two issues caused the greatest difficulty: verification and definition of what constituted a nation's seabed. In its final form, the treaty adoped a 12-mile limit to define the seabed area and agreed on a compromise verification provision. The U.N. General Assembly gave its final approval of the draft on December 7, 1970 and the treaty was subsequently opened for signature in Washington, London, and Moscow on February 11, 1971. It entered into force on May 18, 1972.

The parties to the treaty undertake not to emplant or emplace on the seabed and the ocean floor any nuclear weapons or other types of weapons of mass destruction, as well as structures, launching installations or other facilities specifically designed for storing, testing or using such weapons. They may undertake verification using their own means, with the assistance of other parties, or other appropriate international provisions in accordance with the Charter of the United Nations. Article V binds the parties to "continue negotiations in good faith concerning further measures in the field of disarmament for the prevention of an arms race on the seabed floor and the subsoil thereof."

To this date, 76 nations have deposited instruments of ratification for the Seabed Treaty. An additional 28 states have signed the treaty and have declared themselves bound by its provisions. Two Review Conferences have been held thus far (in 1977 and in 1983) to review operation of the treaty. Both agreed that it is being faithfully observed by all parties.

Senior Arms Control Review Group. This is the senior body and central coordinating mechanism within the United States Government responsible for the development of arms control policy. The Group operates within the National Security Council (NSC) structure from which it receives its guidance and to which it makes its recommendations. On approval by the NSC itself (chaired by the President), the Group's findings and/or recommendations become national policy and are issued to subordinate executive departments and agencies for implementation.

The Senior Arms Control Review Group is composed of senior executives from the Arms Control and Disarmament Agency, the Departments of State and Defense, and the Central Intelligence Agency. The President's Assistant for National Security Affairs (presently Robert McFarlane) chairs the Group's deliberations. The type of issues considered by the Group include arms control policy directives requiring Presidential decision; instructions to U.S. arms control negotiating teams; and reviews of the annual budget and program of the Arms Control and Disarmament Agency.

Soviet Ballistic Missile Defenses. The Soviet Union maintains around Moscow the world's only operational ABM system. It is intended to protect Soviet military and civilian authorities during a nuclear war, rather than provide blanket protection for the city itself. Since 1980, the Soviets have been upgrading and expanding their system within the parameters of the ABM Treaty. The latter limits each side to one ABM site of no more than 100 intercept missiles. (The U.S. ABM site, at Grand Forks, North Dakota, has been on inactive status since 1976.)

Soviet Chemical Weapons. The Soviet Union has the world's largest and best equipped military force for waging chemical warfare. This fact notwithstanding, the Soviet Union continues to pursue a dynamic chemical warfare development program, as evidenced by its continued testing of advanced chemical weapons, the expansion of chemical storage facilities, training of troops, and the continued production of new and advanced agents.

Soviet research and development of militarily useful chemical warfare agents covers a wide range of applications. New chemical agents and combinations of agents are being investigated. A great variety of weapons are on hand, including nerve, blister, choking, and blood. Toxins are also part of the growing Soviet chemical weapons inventory.

Soviet Long-Range Aviation. The Soviet Union has three manned strategic bombers in production or development—the BEAR H, the BACKFIRE and the BLACKJACK.

The BEAR H has been the mainstay of Soviet Long-Range Aviation for nearly two decades. It has capabilities comparable to those of the B-52 and can reach targets at a distance of 8,300 km in unrefueled missions. The BACKFIRE is the most modern Soviet operational bomber and about 30 such aircraft are known to be produced annually. Although limited in range (estimated at about 5,500 km), the BACKFIRE has the operational capability to attack most of the United States in one-way missions. A total of 235 BACKFIRES are in the inventory. Under development is the BLACKJACK which will be larger than the B-1B and somewhat faster. It is expected to reach operational status in 1987.

Space Weapons Control. Several treaties limit arms control in outer space or contain provisions relevant to outer space arms control. The most important of these include the 1967 Outer Space Treaty, which bars deployment in space of nuclear weapons and other weapons of mass destruction; the ABM Treaty; and the SALT agreements, which prohibit interference with National Technical Means of verification (i.e. satellites used to monitor treaty compliance). Despite the existence of these agreements, further arms control measures designed to prevent an arms race in outer space are under study at the U.N. and, bilaterally, by the governments of the United States and of the Soviet Union.

Impetus for the U.N. deliberations was given by the 1981 session of the U.N. General Assembly, which directed the Conference on Disarmament to take up the subject of outer space control. In carrying out this assignment, the Conference has identified the threat posed by antisatellite (ASAT) weapons as the priority issue. However, little additional progress has been made despite extensive debate and the consideration of numerous proposals.

The need to control antisatellite weapons has also been at the forefront of the U.S.-Soviet bilateral talks. Launched in 1977 with great expectations of success, the talks were suspended in December 1979 on news of the Soviet invasion of Afghanistan. Congressional pressure in the intervening years, and a flurry of Soviet proposals urging the resumption of talks proved fruitless, primarily because of the Reagan Administration's belief that an agreement (should it materialize) would be impossible to verify.

Support in the Congress for an ASAT accord has been sustained and bipartisan. Two events have heightened concern in this issue: President Carter's decision in 1977 to develop a U.S. ASAT weapon to counter the Soviet activities in this area, and President Reagan's speech of April 1983 (the STAR WARS speech) which called for research on systems designed to defend the United States against ballistic missiles. To arms control activists, these events (when superimposed on the very ambitious Soviet ASAT activities) had but one meaning: an uncontrolled space arms race was underway, undermining strategic stability worldwide.

As for the Soviet initiatives to resume the ASAT talks, their true purpose has been to derail the development of the U.S. ASAT weapon system. Both the August 1983 Andropov proposal and the July 1984 Chernenko plan called for a moratorium in ASAT weapons development as a precondition of talks. Such a moratorium would prohibit the United States from testing its ASAT system, while not requiring the Soviets to dismantle their ASAT system which is operational and has been flight-tested numerous times.

Special Consultative Group (SCG). This is a NATO forum, established in 1979, to monitor the course of the INF negotiations and to serve as a clearing house for U.S. consultation with the NATO allies on various aspects of arms control negotiations. Since suspension of the INF negotiations in November 1983, the SCG has been largely inactive.

SS-20. A Soviet intermediate-range missile, first deployed in Eastern Europe in 1977, presumably as a replacement for the older SS-4 and SS-5 missiles. Its presence on the European continent gave impetus to the NATO "Dual Track" decision of December 1979.

The SS-20 is mobile, highly accurate, and with a range of

approximately 5,000 kilometers. The missile carries three warheads (the SS-4 and SS-5 missiles have single warheads) and is independently targetable. Current (January 1985) levels are approximately 387 deployed SS-20s, two-thirds of which are able to reach Western Europe. The remainder are targeted on China. The missile depends on a prepared launch site, thus its mobility is somewhat limited. Still, it is extremely difficult to detect when deployed. The SS-20 launcher has the capability of being reloaded and refired.

The U.S. government early in 1985 said the Soviet Union may deploy over the next two years 60 to 100 more SS-20s, for a total of 450 to 500, but by spring Soviet leader Gorbachev said he had "frozen" the SS-20 force level.

Standing Consultative Commission. The Standing Consultative Commission (scc) is a joint U.S./U.S.S.R. body, established on December 21, 1972, following the conclusion of the SALT I agreements. It is charged with promoting implementation of the objectives and provisions of the ABM Treaty and Interim Agreement, as well as the Agreement on the Prevention of Nuclear War. (In Article XVII of the SALT II Treaty, the scc is assigned similar responsibility with respect to that treaty.)

The Commission is responsible for considering questions of compliance with the obligations assumed by the United States and the Soviet Union under the above agreements, for reconciling any misunderstandings or uncertainties arising in the performance of these obligations, and for considering proposals for increasing the viability of the agreements. The United States and the Soviet Union are, each, represented on the scc by a Commissioner, assisted by a staff of advisers and administrative personnel. (General Richard N. Ellis, USAF, was in January 1985 the U.S. Commissioner.) The Commission holds periodic sessions in Geneva at least twice annually (usually in the spring and fall). Proceedings are private.

Star Wars. See **Strategic Defense Initiative (SDI).**

START Talks (Strategic Arms Reduction Talks). The United States and the Soviet Union have been engaged since 1969 in near-ly continual negotiations designed to control strategic nuclear weapons. The only positive results of these negotiations have been the SALT I accords of 1972 (the ABM Treaty, limiting ballistic missile defenses, and the Interim Agreement on strategic offensive arms). Subsequent negotiations toward a more comprehensive agreement culminated in June 1979 with the signing of the SALT II Treaty. This instrument, however, although debated extensively in the Senate, was withdrawn by President Carter from further consideration in the aftermath of the Soviet invasion of Afghanistan.

The START negotiations began in Geneva in June 1982. Underlying their need was the realization that despite the SALT I and II agreements, the nuclear arms race was continuing unabated, adding new and complex dimensions to be resolved. The goal for START, therefore, was to reach an agreement limiting and reducing strategic nuclear weapons and slowing down the competition for strategic arms, through the maintenance of a strategic balance at lower, safer, and less costly levels. The negotiations were suspended by the Soviet Union on December 8, 1983 to "reassess its policies" in view of the discontinuance of the INF negotiations.

Enormous differences separated the United States and Soviet positions during the negotiations. The United States maintained that massive buildups in the Soviet strategic forces, during the past decade, had threatened to affect significantly the strategic balance. The Soviet Union rejected this charge as a U.S. myth designed to reduce the Soviet ICBM force, while leaving the United States free to add new weapons (B-1B, MX, Trident, etc.) to its arsenal.

Although the U.S. position evolved during the START talks, it essentially sought an agreement that would produce significant reductions in the arsenals of *both* sides, result in *equal* levels of arms for both, and be effectively verifiable. The U.S. position was originally outlined by President Reagan in his speech at Eureka College on May 9, 1982. Focus, the President stressed, should be on the most destabilizing systems (i.e. ballistic missiles). His formula called for:

- reduction of ground-based and submarine-based ballistic missiles to equal levels, approximately one-third below current levels (from 8,500 ballistic missile warheads to 5,000 warheads);
- limiting the total deployed ballistic missiles on each side to 850 (roughly one-half the current U.S. inventory);
- as a second phase, placing an equal ceiling on other elements of U.S. and Soviet strategic forces.

(Note that the MX and other advanced U.S. weapons were not on the U.S. agenda.)

The Soviet position was far less ambitious. It called for reductions in all strategic systems, not merely ICBMs as the United States proposed. Specifically, it called for a ceiling on both sides of 1,800 "strategic launchers," consisting of intercontinental ballistic missiles, submarine-launched missile tubes, and intercontinental bombers. The proposal assumed no increase in the number of U.S. "forward-based" strategic weapons (e.g. Pershing), including a ban on long-range ground-launched cruise missiles.

On October 4, 1983, the President modified the United States START position by incorporating into it the "mutual and guaranteed build-down concept" proposed by some members of Congress. Additionally, the United States delegation was authorized by the President to discuss limitations on the airlaunched cruise missiles carried by U.S. bombers and to negotiate tradeoffs "in ways to provide each side maximum flexibility, consistent with a movement toward a more stable balance of forces."

Stealth Bomber. Officially the Advanced Technology Aircraft, the Stealth bomber is being readied for the 1990 time frame. Its greatest advantage over present U.S. aircraft will be its ability to penetrate Soviet defenses by evading radar.

Strategic Defense Initiative (SDI). A Reagan Administration "initiative" (as opposed to a program) designed to build an effective nationwide strategic defense against ballistic missiles. The SDI is popularly known as STAR WARS, because of its high technology, futuristic defense concepts, reminiscent of those employed in the Star Wars movie series.

Initial funding for SDI was approved by the National Security Council in December 1983. It provides for expenditures of $26 billion over a five-year period. Funds slightly under $2 billion were earmarked for FY 1985 activities, mostly for laser research, space surveillance and other relevant technology research and development. No official estimate exists for total SDI expenditures, rumored to be in the hundreds of billions, and neither has a target date been established.

The SDI has few true believers. Critics argue that SDI:

- violates the provisions of the ABM Treaty, which clearly prohibits the "development, testing, and deployment of ABM interceptor missiles";
- will destabilize the strategic balance by prompting the Soviet Union to undertake a similar effort;
- will result in an arms race in space;
- is impossible to achieve on technical grounds (the required technology to make nuclear weapons impotent and obsolete is unattainable);
- does not provide defense against nonmissile threats, such as cruise missiles and bombers.

The SDI supporters concede many of the above arguments but support the concept, anyway, as the only foolproof means of ever determining whether a workable defense against missiles is possible.

Strategic Offensive Forces. Both the United States and the Soviet Union rely on "triads" of strategic forces to deter the other side from aggression. A "triad" consists of three different types of delivery systems: land-based missiles, submarines, and airplanes. The basic purpose of a triad is to complicate the opponent's defenses and to guarantee that some of one's systems will always survive a surprise attack and be available for a counter-attack.

The U.S. strategic offensive forces consist of:
- 1,033 ICBMs (1,000 Minuteman and 33 Titan missiles);
- 320 strategic bombers (260 B-52s and 60 FB-111s); and
- 616 fleet ballistic launchers (496 Poseidons and 120 Trident Is).

Collectively, the United States triad accounts for about 11,000 warheads. Planned acquisitions during the 1980s include 100 MX missiles, 100 B-1B bombers, and unknown quantities of Midgetman missiles, Stealth bombers, and Trident II (D 5) ballistic missile launchers.

The Soviet strategic offensive forces consist of:
- 1,400 ICBMs;
- 145 strategic bombers; and
- 980 fleet ballistic launchers.

Total warheads are estimated at 8,200. Three missile systems (SS-X-24, SS-X-25, and SS-NX-23) and an advanced bomber (the BLACKJACK) are under development.

Threshold Test Ban Treaty. The "Treaty on Underground Nuclear Weapon Tests," also known as the Threshold Test Ban Treaty (TTBT), was signed in Moscow on July 3, 1974. It establishes a nuclear "threshold" by prohibiting tests of a yield greater than 150 kilotons (equivalent to 150,000 tons of TNT). The threshold is militarily important for it places a restraint on the explosive force of nuclear warheads and bombs.

The TTBT is the second arms control accord, between the United States and the Soviet Union, involving limitations in nuclear testing. In 1963, they, along with the United Kingdom, signed the Limited Test Ban Treaty (still in effect) which prohibits nuclear testing in the atmosphere, in outer space, and under water. The Limited Test Ban Treaty bans also nuclear explosions in other environments (e.g. underground) that would cause radioactive debris to be present beyond the borders of the country in which the explosion took place. Underground tests, however, are not explicitly prohibited by the 1963 treaty.

Agreement on the TTBT was reached during the summit meeting in Moscow in July 1974. The treaty includes a protocol which describes the technical data to be exchanged and which limits weapon testing to specific designated test sites to assist verification. The TTBT was forwarded to the United States Senate for ratification, in July 1976, where it is still awaiting action. The Reagan Administration has repeatedly stated that it is not pleased with the treaty's verification provisions and that it wishes parts of it renegotiated. The Soviet Union has refused to discuss any changes, declaring that the treaty had been negotiated and signed in good faith and that, therefore, any amendments would have to await ratification in the United States Senate.

Under the terms of the treaty, each nation agrees to:

- prohibit, prevent, and not carry out underground nuclear weapon tests having a yield exceeding 150 kilotons;
- limit the number of its underground nuclear weapon tests to a minimum; and,
- continue negotiations toward solution to the problem of the cessation of all underground nuclear weapon tests.

Assurance of compliance is by National Technical Means of verification, with each party undertaking not to interfere with the operation of such systems. The provisions of the treaty do not extend to underground nuclear explosions carried out for peaceful purposes. These are covered by a separate treaty (refer to next entry).

A Protocol to the TTBT requires the signatory nations to exchange the following data for purposes of further verification of compliance:

- the geographic coordinates of the boundaries of each nuclear test site;
- the geology of the testing areas of the sites;
- the geographic coordinates of underground nuclear weapon tests, after they have been conducted; and,
- yield, date, time, depth and coordinates for two nuclear weapons tests from each geophysically distinct testing area where tests have been or are to be conducted.

On September 24, 1984, in his address to the U.N. General Assembly, President Reagan called upon the Soviet Union to agree to the exchange of visits by experts to nuclear test sites "to measure directly the yields of tests of nuclear weapons."

Treaty on Underground Nuclear Explosions for Peaceful Purposes. While negotiating the Threshold Test Ban Treaty (TTBT), the United States and the Soviet Union recognized the need to establish a parallel agreement to govern underground nuclear explosions for "peaceful purposes." Such agreement was needed because no essential distinction could be made between the technology of a nuclear explosive device which could be used as a weapon and that used for a peaceful purpose. Negotiations began in Moscow, resulting in the "Treaty of Underground Nuclear Explosions for Peaceful Purposes" (PNE Treaty). Signed on May 28, 1976, the agreement consists of three parts: the Treaty proper, a detailed Protocol, and an Agreed Statement.

Each party undertakes to prohibit, to prevent and not to carry out at any place under its jurisdiction or control:

- an individual explosion having a yield exceeding 150 kilotons;
- a group explosion (consisting of a number of individual explosions) having an aggregate yield exceeding one and one-half megatons;
- a group explosion having an aggregate yield exceeding 150 kilotons, unless the individual explosions in the group could be identified and measured by agreed verification procedures;
- an explosion which does not carry out a peaceful application.

The parties reserve the right to carry out nuclear explosions for peaceful purposes in the territory of another country, if requested to do so, but only in full compliance with the yield limitations and other provisions of the PNE Treaty and in accord with the Non-Proliferation Treaty. Verification is by National Technical Means, information exchange, and access to sites of explosions.

The Protocol to the PNE Treaty sets forth the specific arrangements to be followed for assuring that no weapon-related benefits, precluded by the TTBT, are derived by carrying out nuclear explosions for peaceful purposes. It includes provisions for detailed information to be exchanged and the rights and functions of observers. The Agreed Statement which accompanies the PNE Treaty precludes "development testing of nuclear explosives" as being considered "peaceful applications." Any such development tests must be carried out in accordance with the provisions of the TTBT.

The PNE Treaty was forwarded to the U.S. Senate for ratification in July 1976, where it is still awaiting action. As in the case with the TTBT, the Reagan Administration is not pleased with some of the treaty's verification provisions and wishes them renegotiated. The

Soviet Union has refused to discuss any changes, declaring that the treaty had been negotiated and signed in good faith and that, therefore, any amendments would have to await U.S. Senate ratification.

Trident. The term is used both for the submarine and its associated ballistic missile.

Trident submarines are the latest and most modern strategic system in the U.S. nuclear arsenal. They are larger, faster, and quieter and carry more missiles than their predecessors (24 tubes on the Trident vs. 16 on the Poseidon). As of early 1985, four Trident submarines are in service and eight others are under construction. Eventually, the entire Poseidon submarine force (31 boats) will be replaced.

Trident missiles are in two configurations: Trident I is deployed and fully operational; Trident II (also known as D 5) is in full-scale engineering development, with deployment expected in late 1989. It will have a longer range, greater accuracy, and higher yield than Trident I. Present unofficial reports place the number of warheads per D 5 missile at 10–14; i.e. one Trident II submarine will carry 24 missiles with up to 336 warheads (an awesome amount of power by any standard).

The Trident system acquisition cost for a force of 15 submarines is estimated at approximately $70 billion. Indications are that a force of 20 Trident submarines is being sought, at a program cost of $85 billion.

Umbrella Talks. This is the unofficial designation given to the preliminary talks held in Geneva, January 7–8, 1985, between Secretary of State George Shultz and Soviet Foreign Secretary Andrei Gromyko on the subject of future U.S.-Soviet arms control negotiations. During the course of these talks, the two sides agreed that the subject of the future negotiations will be a "complex of questions concerning space and nuclear arms, both strategic and intermediate range, with all questions considered and resolved in their interrelationship." The negotiations will be conducted by one delegation from each side divided into three groups (i.e. one each for strategic weapons, intermediate range weapons, and space weapons).

As a concession to the Soviet Union, the planned negotiations are being referred to as "new", to remove the implication that the Soviets are returning to the negotiating table which they abandoned late in 1983. The United States also agreed to a "linkage" between the three sets of talks as a concession to the Soviets who reportedly consider U.S. space activities (ASATs, Star Wars, the Space Shuttle) as a major threat to their security. Unless the United States agrees to limitations in these systems, the Soviet Union will balk at any agreement reducing strategic and intermediate range forces.

President Reagan has named Max M. Kampelman to head the U.S. delegation in these future talks and also to be chief negotiator on the space issues. Ex-Senator John G. Tower will be chief negotiator on strategic or long-range nuclear arms. A career diplomat, Maynard W. Glitman, will be chief negotiator on medium-range forces in Europe.

United Kingdom. Nuclear Forces. In comparison to those of the superpowers, the nuclear forces of the U.K. are fairly limited. They consist of four Polaris A-3 submarines and 64 Vulkan IRBMs. The U.K., however, is on the verge of a very ambitious nuclear modernization program, including the replacement during the 1990s of its Polaris fleet with Trident II (D 5) submarines and missiles. If plans materialize, the U.K. will possess a superpower capability of nearly 1,000 warheads, sufficient to eliminate the Soviet Union as a power.

Soviet concern over the increasing U.K. nuclear capabilities became apparent during the Intermediate-Range Nuclear Forces (INF) negotiations in Geneva. The Soviet Union demanded that these forces be included in the agenda of the negotiations. The United States maintained, throughout, that the INF forum was "bilateral" (i.e. between the United States and the Soviet Union), and that therefore, discussion of the British and French nuclear forces was inappropriate.

United Nations. Disarmament Commission. Composed of all U.N. members, it was created in 1951 as a deliberative rather than ne-gotiating body dealing with issues of disarmament. Having fallen into disuse, it was reactivated in 1978 by the First Special Session on Disarmament of the U.N. General Assembly. It has since been meeting in New York City, usually in May and June of each year. The Commission operates under its own rules of procedure and reports to the U.N. General Assembly.

In recent sessions, the Commission has focused primarily on elements of the Comprehensive Program on Disarmament and on various proposals for the reduction of military budgets. During its 1983 session, it deliberated also on the nuclear capability of South Africa and on the subject of "confidence building measures."

U.N. General Assembly. Since its inception, the U.N. General Assembly has taken a keen interest in arms control and disarmament matters, expressing its views through resolutions, commissioning studies on arms control topics, and often suggesting areas for possible arms control negotiation. Resolutions are debated and voted upon within its "First Committee," which is responsible, exclusively, for disarmament and related international security questions.

Although other U.N. bodies are also concerned with disarmament issues, the General Assembly remains the ultimate U.N. instrumentality in this area. All draft disarmament conventions negotiated by the Conference on Disarmament are submitted to the Assembly for review and approval, prior to their presentation to member states for signature.

Annually, a large number of arms control related resolutions are debated and voted upon within the Assembly. The earliest such resolution on record, dated January 24, 1946, sought the elimination of atomic weapons and assurance that atomic energy would be used for peaceful purposes.

In 1983, a total of 62 resolutions on various disarmament matters were passed. They covered such topics as the cessation of the arms race, the prohibition of nuclear testing, a freeze on nuclear weapons, the creation of new nuclear-weapon-free-zones, elimination of chemical and bacteriological weapons, and the reduction of military budgets.

U.N. General Assembly, Special Sessions on Disarmament. "Special Sessions on Disarmament" are held by the U.N. General Assembly at four-year intervals. Their purpose is to give momentum to the disarmament movement and to provide a forum for world leaders to express their concerns over the arms race and the threat of nuclear war. Two such sessions have been held to date.

- *First Session* (23 May to 1 July 1978): This was the largest and most representative meeting ever to consider the world's disarmament problems. All U.N. member states participated, many at the highest levels of government. The session adopted a 129-paragraph Final Document which provides the framework for the international community's disarmament efforts in the years ahead. The Document includes a "Program of Action" and also establishes and defines the structure and machinery for disarmament within the U.N.
- *Second Session* (June 7 to July 10, 1982): As in the case of the First Session, all U.N. member states participated, including 18 heads of state or governments and 44 foreign ministers. Several draft resolutions were debated, containing proposals for a nuclear arms freeze; the prevention of nuclear war; prohibition on the uses of nuclear weapons; and urgent

measures for nuclear disarmament. Unfortunately, the session ended without agreement, its only accomplishment being the launching of a World Disarmament Campaign and an increase in the number of U.N. fellowships on disarmament.

U.N. Headquarters, Department of Disarmament Affairs. The Department of Disarmament Affairs (formerly the U.N. Center for Disarmament) is the world organization's principal headquarters activity for disarmament affairs. The Department serves as an information clearing house for all disarmament developments carried out under U.N. auspices (unilateral, bilateral, regional, or multilateral); coordinates and provides logistical support to U.N. conferences dealing with disarmament issues; and manages the U.N. program of "Fellowships on Disarmament." The Department maintains an aggressive publications program, which includes *The U.N. Disarmament Yearbook*; the periodical *Disarmament*; the *Fact Sheet* series; and the *Disarmament Study* series.

United States. Chemical Weapons. Under the terms of the Geneva Convention of 1925, nations are prohibited from "using" chemical weapons in warfare. The convention, however, does not prohibit the production or stockpiling of such weapons. Accordingly, chemical agents continue to be maintained in the arsenals of numerous nations, including the United States.

The United States has not produced chemical weapons since 1969. The Reagan Administration has repeatedly sought permission from the Congress to do so; however, all these requests have been denied. The Administration maintains that existing U.S. chemical weapons are becoming rapidly obsolete and that they cannot be relied upon to perform efficiently on the battlefield. The Administration also justifies its requests for new chemical weapons in terms of the need to maintain a credible deterrent, and to redress the imbalance that has developed as a result of the continued Soviet expansion and modernization of its chemical weapons.

Opponents of renewed U.S. chemical weapons production argue that existing stocks are sufficient for deterrence. Supporters argue that their absence could force the United States to respond with nuclear weapons in the event of Soviet chemical attack, thus causing a nuclear escalation in a situation not requiring it.

U.S. Congress. Role in Arms Control. The powers of the Congress for foreign relations, and accordingly for arms control, are derived from the Constitution of the United States, specifically: Sections 1, 8, and 9 of Article I, and Sections 1 and 2 of Article II. These powers are carried out by the various Congressional Committees, eight such Committees playing especially prominent roles in the area of arms control:

- Senate Foreign Relations Committee
- Senate Armed Services Committee
- Senate Appropriations Committee
- Senate Select Committee on Intelligence
- House Foreign Affairs Committee
- House Armed Services Committee
- House Appropriations Committee
- House Select Committee on Intelligence

Although the specific responsibilities carried out by the above committees vary, the principal thrust of congressional arms control activity is in four areas:

- recommending "advice and consent" on treaties and other international agreements (carried out exclusively by the Senate Foreign Relations Committee);
- considering legislative proposals, resolutions, etc.;
- considering appropriations requests by the U.S. Arms Control and Disarmament Agency;
- performing oversight functions, such as monitoring treaty compliance and verification (carried out principally by the Intelligence Committees).

U.S.-Soviet Joint Working Groups. This is the designation given to six U.S.-Soviet Working Groups which were established in 1977 for the purpose of addressing six specific arms control initiatives: anti-satellite systems, chemical weapons, the demilitarization of the Indian Ocean, radiological weapons, conventional arms transfers, and a comprehensive nuclear test ban.

The levels of activity of these working groups has varied through the years. Some, such as the Antisatellite Systems Joint Working Group, have not met in several years. Others meet rarely.

Verification. Verification entails a two-step process. Prior to the negotiation of an arms control agreement, it must forecast whether the other side could evade detection should it attempt to violate the agreement in a manner detrimental to national security. After the agreement has been negotiated and signed, verification must determine on a near-continuous basis the extent to which provisions are being complied with.

Profound policy differences separate the United States and Soviet verification policies. The U.S. policy heavily emphasizes that an arms control agreement concluded with the Soviet Union must be verifiable or there can be no agreement at all. Underlying this policy is a continuing distrust of the Russians and the fear that, somewhere along the way, they might trick the United States into disarming itself unilaterally. In contrast, the Soviet Union sees no need for special verification provisions in an arms control agreement. Compliance, in its view, can be assured by the pressure of public opinion. A nation simply would have no incentive to violate an arms accord and in the process invite upon it the wrath of all the nations.

Verification provisions in existing arms control agreements vary from *no* provisions whatever (as in the case of the Seabed Arms Control Treaty and the Biological Convention) to the very generous verification terms included in the Antarctic Treaty. During the past decade, emphasis has been placed increasingly on NTM as vehicles of verification. U.S. proposals for additional verification, such as for on-site inspection of key sites, have been summarily rejected by the Soviet leadership as ploys designed to spy on the Soviet Union.

Walk in the Woods Formula. A series of private discussions during July 1982 between ambassadors Paul Nitze (U.S.) and Yuli Kvitsinsky at the Intermediate-Range Nuclear Forces (INF) negotiations. Purpose was to develop a mutually acceptable formula, not constrained by formally tabled positions, for reducing U.S. and Soviet INF in Europe. The negotiators agreed, that the package developed during "informal walks in the woods" did not constitute an offer on behalf of either government. Rather, it represented an initiative of two Ambassadors working as individuals.

The package developed by ambassadors Nitze and Kvitsinsky contained the following points:

- the United States and Soviet Union would each be limited to 75 intermediate-range missile launchers in Europe (including the Soviet SS-20s on the eastern slopes of the Urals);
- each side would be limited to only 150 intermediate-range aircraft in Europe;
- within its limit, the United States would deploy in Europe cruise missiles only, not Pershings II;
- the Soviet Union would be limited to 90 intermediate-range missile launchers in the eastern Soviet Union;
- each allowed ballistic missile launcher would carry no more than 1 missile and no more than 3 warheads;

- each allowed ground-launched cruise missile would carry no more than 4 missiles, each with no more than 1 warhead;
- all intermediate-range missiles systems in excess of the above limits would be destroyed.

The Nitze-Kvitsinsky formula has been officially rejected by both the U.S. and Soviet Governments, for fear that the other side might consider it a formal proposal. Still, numerous, observors consider the formula the most promising framework for a future INF agreement.

World Military Expenditures. According to studies completed by U.S. and U.N. organizations, the world's military expenditures amount to $970 billion annually, or approximately $200 for each man, woman and child on earth. Additional major study findings include:

- Fifty million persons are directly or indirectly engaged in military activities worldwide. Of this total, approximately one-half serve in the military forces of various nations, while millions of others serve in para-military forces.
- Approximately 20% of the world's qualified scientists and engineers are engaged in military-related activities. At least five million workers are employed in plants producing weapons of various kinds.
- The use of petroleum for military purposes, including its indirect consumption in military industry, is estimated at 5 to 6% of the total global consumption.
- More than 37 billion dollars is annually traded in arms traffic, by both developed and developing countries.

World Disarmament Campaign. This campaign, launched by the U.N. General Assembly on June 7, 1982, is designed to inform, educate, and generate public understanding and support for the objectives of the United Nations in the field of disarmament. The campaign is global in scope.

Participation in the World Disarmament Campaign is by both governmental and nongovernmental organizations, academic institutions, and research institutes. Activities include publications, seminars, conferences, meetings, photo and art exhibits and public rallies. The convening of several regional conferences is also planned. The first such conferences were held in New Delhi in August 1983 and in Leningrad in June 1984.

Part II
Organizations Active
in Arms Control/Disarmament
(U.S. and Foreign)

American Enterprise Institute, 1150 17th Street, NW, Washington, DC 20036. The American Enterprise Institute is a nonprofit, nonpartisan, publicly supported research and educational organization. Its purpose is to assist scholars, businessmen, policy makers, the press, and the public by providing objective analyses of national and international issues. (Arms control and disarmament are among the key issues analyzed by the Institute under its "National Defense Studies" program.)

Principal Activities: Undertakes research on a great variety of public policy issues, including arms control. Publishes findings in a large number of reviews, journals and newsletters. Principal issues studied include: National Defense; Economic Policy; Energy Policy; Education Policy; International Affairs; Religion, Philosophy; Government Regulations; Health Policy; Legal Policy; Political and Social Processes; Fiscal Policy; and Public Policy.

Major Publications: Public Opinion (bimonthly magazine), *Regulation* (bimonthly magazine), *AEI Economist* (monthly newsletter), and *AEI Foreign Policy and Defense Review* (bimonthly). For a listing of the latest AEI titles refer to *AEI Publications Catalog*.

American Friends Service Committee, 1501 Cherry Street, Philadelphia, PA 19102. The Committee is dedicated to building informed resistance to war and militarism and advancing nonviolent action for change. It maintains offices in Atlanta, Baltimore, Cambridge, Chicago, Dayton, Des Moines, New York, Pasadena, Seattle, and San Francisco.

Principal Activities: The Committee maintains an active educational program supporting a U.S.–Soviet nuclear weapons freeze and against U.S. deployment of Pershing II and cruise missiles in Europe.

Major Publications: Very extensive collection of publications on the above issues. Also publishes the AFSC *Quaker Service Bulletin* (quarterly).

Arms Control Association, 11 Dupont Circle, NW, Washington, DC 20036. The Association is a nonpartisan national membership organization dedicated to promoting public understanding of effective policies and programs in arms control and disarmament. It seeks to create broad public appreciation of the need for positive steps toward the limitation of armaments and the implementation of other measures to reduce international tensions on the road to world peace.

Principal Activities: Publishes *Arms Control Today*, a highly regarded compendium of opinion analysis and factual information on arms control issues. Provides speakers for civic, educational, and community groups and sponsors educational materials and training for teachers. Testifies before Congressional committees and other forums considering arms control and disarmament proposals. Sponsors regular press briefings, meetings and conferences with national leaders. Provides research and information assistance to scholars, students and institutions.

Major Publications: Arms Control Today (monthly) and *World Military and Social Expenditures* (annual). Numerous additional book titles dealing with arms control issues are available for purchase from the Association.

The Bertrand Russell Peace Foundation, Bertrand Russell House, Gamble Street, Nottingham, United Kingdom. The Foundation was formed in 1963 to carry forward Russell's work for peace, human rights and social justice. It seeks to identify and counter the causes of war and violence and to promote research into disarmament. Overseas branches of the foundation are active in Australia, France, and Japan.

Principal Activities: Conducts research and publishes scholarly papers on the peaceful settlement of disputes and disarmament issues. Hosts international seminars and, in the past, has organized "Russell Tribunals" designed to draw attention to injustices in various parts of the world. The Foundation is presently active in the campaign for European nuclear disarmament.

Major Publications: All foundation publications carry the imprint SPOKESMAN. Hundreds of titles have been published in the form of books, pamphlets and journals.

Brookings Institution, 1775 Massachusetts Avenue, NW, Washington, DC 20036. Brookings is a private nonprofit organization devoted to research, education, and publication of important issues of domestic and foreign policy. Its principal purpose is to bring knowledge to bear on the current and emerging policy problems facing the American people. (Arms control and disarmament are investigated extensively by the Institution under its "Foreign Policy Studies" program.)

Principal Activities: Subjects are selected for study on the basis of their significance and timeliness, the adequacy of information, availability of personnel and funds, and the relationship to the Institution's objectives. Completed studies are offered as scholarly treatment of a topic worthy of public consideration; the Institution itself does not take position on policy issues.

Major Publications: Selected Brookings publications in print, and others in preparation, are listed in a quarterly publication entitled *Brookings Books* (date). Publishes also the *Brookings Review* (quarterly).

Business Executives for National Security, Euram Bldg., 21 Dupont Circle, NW, Suite 401, Washington, DC 20036. This is an organization of business executives, entrepreneurs, and self-employed professionals who seek to promote genuine national security by working for "practical, cost-effective alternatives to the current massive and economically-harmful arms build-up." The organization supports a U.S. military which is sufficient to counter the threat posed by the Soviet Union, but is on record as favoring a policy of nonuse of nuclear weapons.

Principal Activities: Produces and disseminates *Congressional Action Alerts* and *Fact Sheets* on upcoming issues on Capitol Hill, operates a Speakers Bureau, and sponsors meetings and events which address issues of concern to the organization. Operates also the "Business Executives for National Security Education Fund."

Major Publications: Business and National Security Trendline (newsletter).

Canadian Centre for Arms Control and Disarmament, 151 Slater Street, Ottawa, Ontario, Canada. The Center was established to encourage informed debate and to provide Canadians with independent, nonpartisan research and reliable information relating to arms control and disarmament.

Principal Activities: The Center pursues research and education and information programs. The research program encompasses a broad spectrum of research activities on problems of international arms control, military technology, and the role of force in international affairs. Findings are presented and distributed through the *Aurora Papers*, a series of occasional publications. The Center's education and information program consists of the publication, bimonthly, of the *Arms Control Chronicle* and of other reports, and of seminars intended to generate thinking on arms control issues.

Major Publications: The *Aurora Papers* and the *Arms Control Chronicle.*

Carnegie Endowment for International Peace, 11 Dupont Circle, NW, Washington, DC 20036 or 30 Rockefeller Plaza, New York, NY 10112. An operating (not a grant-making) foundation, the Carnegie Endowment for International Peace conducts its own programs of research, discussion, publication, and education in international affairs and American foreign policy. Although program emphasis changes periodically, the Endowment has devoted substantial attention through the years to the study of arms control. An important part of this effort is the Endowment's joint venture relationship with the Arms Control Association.

Principal Activities (only arms control/disarmament activities are listed): Conducts research and publishes scholarly treatise on arms control and disarmament issues. Hosts the "Carnegie Panel on U.S. Security and the Future of Arms Control," a nonpartisan panel which explores contributions that arms control might make to U.S. security. Sponsors unofficial international meetings to preview/review prospects and/or progress at official arms control conferences.

Major Publications: Publishes *Foreign Policy*, a prestigious quarterly journal of foreign policy.

Center for Defense Information, 600 Maryland Avenue, SW, Washington, DC 20024. The Center is a nonprofit, nonpartisan, research organization that supports a strong defense, but opposes excesses and waste in military spending and programs that increase the danger of nuclear war. The Center is a project of the *Fund for Peace.*

Principal Activities: Provides facts to citizens and decision-makers about growing military budgets and new weapons systems. Lobbies on Capitol Hill for arms control and against specific weapons systems (i.e., MX, cruise missiles). Has produced "War Without Winners," a nationally televised film warning of the dangers of nuclear war.

Major Publications: Defense Monitor (monthly) and *Nuclear*

War Prevention Kit. Numerous additional publications on specific arms control issues.

Citizens Against Nuclear War, 1201 Sixteenth Street, NW, Washington, DC 20036. This is a coalition of over fifty national membership organizations that "share a deep concern for the survival of our planet." Members include religious organizations, labor unions, women's groups, environmental organizations, civil rights groups and professional associations. (No individual memberships are offered.) The coalition seeks the following objectives: implementation of a verifiable, bilateral freeze; cancellation of civil defense plans to evacuate American cities; observance of all previously negotiated international agreements; and negotiation of additional agreements to reduce the risk of war.

Principal Activities: Provides support services to member organizations, including: assistance in developing articles for journals and newsletters; provision of timely legislative alerts and updates; and speech writing assistance. Assists member organizations in sponsoring "Community Education Forums" on aspects of nuclear arms control and the prevention of nuclear war.

Clergy and Laity Concerned (CALC), 198 Broadway, Room 302, New York, NY 10038. This is a peace and justice organization which concentrates on two major areas of concern: disarmament and economic justice; and human rights and racial justice. Founded in 1965 to mobilize the religious community against the war in Vietnam, the organization consists today of a network of 51 chapters and action groups in 31 states.

Principal Activities: Clergy and Laity Concerned supports a bilateral freeze of nuclear weapons, a nuclear-free Pacific, and the conversion of nuclear weapon facilities to useful purposes. It works also to bring about an end to the U.S. support of South Africa's nuclear program. In the past, CALC has participated in the campaigns against the MX missile and the B-1 bomber and for greater U.S. appreciation of the European peace movements.

Major Publications: CALC publications include the *CALC Report* (monthly); the *Arms Race Is Already Killing*; and *Pershing II and Cruise Missiles: Spreading Chaos*.

Coalition for a New Foreign and Military Policy, 712 G Street SE, Washington, DC 20003. This is a coalition of over 50 national, peace, professional, and social organizations dedicated to the development of a "peaceful, noninterventionist, and demilitarized foreign policy for the United States." Specifically, the coalition supports and works for arms control and disarmament and the conversion of defense-dependent sectors of the U.S. economy to civilian, peacetime production; shifting U.S. spending from excessive military programs to human need programs; support of human rights and the termination of U.S. aid to repressive foreign governments.

Principal Activities: The coalition analyzes key issues in U.S. foreign and military policy and coordinates and focuses the educational and lobbying efforts of its member organizations toward these issues. It produces and distributes educational resources (fact sheets, pamphlets, legislative updates), and organizes citizens' actions in support of the coalition's goals.

Major Publications: Coalition Close-Up (newsletter) and various *Action Guides* and *Action Alerts* on pending legislation. Publishes *Annual Voting Record* on key House and Senate votes.

The Committee for National Security, 2000 P Street, NW, Suite 515, Washington, DC 20036. The Committee for National Security is a nonprofit, nonpartisan citizen's organization concerned with the dangers caused by the excessive U.S. reliance on military solutions to complex foreign policy problems. It seeks to educate the public that security is not served by an uncontrolled accumulation of nuclear weapons. To lessen the risk of nuclear war, these weapons must be reduced "through prudent and verifiable arms limitation agreements."

Principal Activities: The Committee has an active educational program consisting of regional and national conferences on national security issues, and the sponsorship of courses on current arms control topics (military budget, U.S.–Soviet negotiations, etc.). It organizes outreach activities, including press and Congressional briefings, and produces publicity materials on national security issues.

Major Publications: CNS Report (newsletter), *Issue Briefs*, and *Conference Proceedings*.

Common Cause, 2030 M Street, NW, Washington, DC 20036. Common Cause is a nonprofit, nonpartisan citizen's lobby working for open and effective government. Its agenda covers numerous national issues. In the area of arms control, the organization supports:

- an immediate, verifiable freeze on the production, testing, and deployment of nuclear weapons;
- substantial reductions in U.S. and Soviet nuclear forces;
- adoption of a policy of no first use of nuclear weapons;
- strengthening national and international control to prevent the spread of nuclear weapons;

- negotiation of a comprehensive test ban treaty;
- banning anti-satellite weapons and the placement of military weapons in space; and
- a military posture that gives neither the Soviet Union nor the United States an incentive to launch a first strike.

The organization is financed entirely from dues and contributions of its members (250,000 nationwide).

Principal Activities: Works to educate the public-at-large on the consequences of nuclear war and marshals its support on the above arms control issues. Lobbies extensively on Capitol Hill, provides expert testimony before Congressional Committees, and publishes a newsletter alerting members to impending Congressional action. Sponsors meetings, conferences, and symposia on critical arms control issues.

Major Publications: Common Cause (a bimonthly political magazine), *Citizens Action Guide*, and *Hot Line* (A Nuclear Arms Alert Network Newsletter).

Council for a Livable World, National Office: 11 Beacon Street, Boston, MA 02108. Legislative Office: 100 Maryland Avenue, NE, Washington, DC 20002. Purpose of the Council is to warn the public and the Congress of the threat of nuclear war and to lead the way to rational arms control.

Principal Activities: Monitors and influences arms control legislation in the U.S. Senate. Provides Senators with information to help them make intelligent decisions on nuclear arms control and strategic weapons. Maintains a Political Action Committee to help elect to the Senate men and women who support serious nuclear arms control. A separate Political Action Committee (Peace PAC) makes campaign contributions to candidates for the U.S. House of Representatives who vigorously support nuclear arms control. Operates an Education Fund (to help educate Americans about the consequences of nuclear war), a Legislative Alert Network (for grassroots lobbying aimed at important legislative battles) and a Nuclear Arms Control Hotline (202/543–0006) which provides the latest information on arms control and military budget legislation.

Major Publications: Fact Sheets on various weapons systems and/or arms control issues. Publishes also an *Annual Voting Record* for all members of the Congress.

Educators for Social Responsibility, 23 Garden Street, Cambridge, MA 02138. This is a national, nonprofit membership organization consisting of parents, teachers, and school administrators dedicated to "educating students on issues relating to the nuclear arms race." Goal is a world free from the threat of nuclear destruction. Maintains 90 chapters in 35 states. Total membership is 5,500.

Principal Activities: Prepares and distributes educational materials designed to inform on the risks of the continuing arms race and the threat of nuclear war. Operates a National Resource Center which supports teacher training, curriculum development, research, and implementation of balanced curricula in schools.

Major Publications: Curricula, annotated bibliographies, and audiovisual materials on nuclear war and on the means for promoting and preserving peace. Publishes *FORUM*, a quarterly of new ideas relating to nuclear education.

Ford Foundation, 320 East 43rd Street, New York, NY 10017. The Ford Foundation is a private nonprofit institution serving the public welfare. It works mainly by providing funds to other institutions and organizations for activities that show promise in solving problems of national and international importance. In some instances, the Foundation makes also grants to individuals whose professional talent or experience corresponds with its programs and activities. "International affairs" issues, which include arms control and international security, are one of the six major themes of the Foundation's program.

Principal Activities (only arms control/disarmament activities are listed): Sponsors international competitions for research on international security and arms control, and funds scholarly research on a variety of arms control topics. Provides grants to prestigious institutes (both U.S. and foreign) to develop information and assessments on key worldwide military and strategic developments, the economic consequences of defense spending, and the security concerns of smaller nations.

Major Publications: Publications are listed in *Ford Foundation Publications and Films*.

Friends of the Earth, 530 7th Street, SE, Washington, DC 20003. This is primarily an environmental lobby which argues for "restraint and respect for all living things." It supports nuclear arms control and a mutually verifiable bilateral nuclear freeze as a means of protecting the environment. Publishes *Not Man Apart*, a monthly journal.

Greenpeace, U.S.A., 2007 R Street, NW, Washington, DC 20009. Greenpeace is an international organization currently active in fifteen countries. The group, established in 1971, is involved in a broad range of issues to protect the global environment (with particular emphasis on nuclear disarmament), ocean ecology, wildlife protection, and the control of toxic substances. The conclusion of a Comprehensive Nuclear Test Ban Treaty is a major goal.

Principal Activities: Greenpeace employs nonviolent direct action, including lobbying, public education, and mobilization of citizens to accomplish its goals. Among its accomplishments, Greenpeace lists the end of underground nuclear testing on Amchitka Island in Alaska; the termination of French H-bomb testing in the South Pacific; the passage of legislation in the U.S. Senate calling for an immediate resumption of U.S./Soviet test ban treaty negotiations; and reversal by the Navy of its plan to scuttle nuclear sub reactor cores in U.S. coastal waters.

Major Publications: Preventing Nuclear War and *The Case for a Comprehensive Test Ban Treaty*.

Ground Zero, 806 15th Street, NW, Suite 421, Washington, DC 20005. Ground Zero is a nonpartisan, nonadvocacy organization that works to educate the American people about the threat of nuclear war and to involve them in efforts to prevent it. Ground Zero does not lobby for any particular political approach to reducing the threat of nuclear war. Instead, it focuses on creating an informed citizenry that is a prerequisite for enabling a solution to this complex issue.

Principal Activities: Activities are educational in nature. Achieved national prominence in April 1982, when it organized Ground Zero Week in over 600 cities across the country. Sponsored "What About the Russians Week" in April 1983. Has recently formed the "Ground Zero Pairing Project" which organizes outreach programs from U.S. citizens and students to their Soviet counterparts. Promotes "Nuclear War Firebreaks" and "Let's Make a Deal," war/peace games.

Major Publications: Has published two widely acclaimed paper back books, *Nuclear War: What's in It for You?* and *What About the Russians—and Nuclear War?* Also, curriculum guides, minicourses, debate packages, posters, slide shows, and bibliographies. Distributes monthly newsletter, *Report from Ground Zero*.

High Technology Professionals for Peace, 639 Massachusetts Avenue, Room 316, Cambridge, MA 02139. This is a nonprofit organization of scientists, engineers, and other technical professionals concerned with the threat of nuclear war. Purpose is to provide information about the impact of weapons systems on national security, the economy, the environment, and society. The organization supports the Nuclear Freeze Campaign and other initiatives designed to halt the nuclear arms race.

Principal Activities: Emphasis is on the desirability of professionals shifting from military to nonmilitary employment. Toward this goal, the organization promotes discussion forums involving work in the defense industry, and also operates a nonprofit employment agency to offer engineers and scientists alternatives to weapons-related work.

Major Publications: Technology and Responsibility (a quarterly newsletter).

Hudson Institute, Quaker Ridge Road, Croton-on-Hudson, NY 10520. The Hudson Institute examines issues of policy that lie in the public interest, primarily in the areas of national security, international affairs, economics, education, and social and cultural trends. A not-for-profit corporation, Hudson draws its members from business, the military, academia, and the political community. Arms control issues are explored as a component of studies on "National Security and the International Order."

Principal Activities: The Institute pursues a wide variety of national security subjects on behalf of the U.S. and NATO governments, private corporations and foundation clients. Research is conducted inhouse by means of a cadre of scientists and through the Center for Naval Analyses. The latter organization operates as a division of the Hudson Institute and conducts operations research, systems analysis, and management science for the Navy and the Marine Corps.

Institute for Defense and Disarmament Studies, 2001 Beacon Street, Brookline, MA 02146. The Institute is a center for research and public education. It studies the nature and purposes of military forces to identify obstacles to and opportunities for disarmament. Its main research projects aim to delineate trends in worldwide military forces, to survey current military and arms control policies, and to develop safer and more defensively-oriented policies which would lead to a global reduction of armaments. The Institute was the founder of the nuclear freeze proposal.

Principal Activities: Supports key arms control initiatives (such as the U.S.–Soviet nuclear weapons freeze) through the preparation and distribution of publicity materials; participation in public debates; and testimony before Congressional panels and committees. Hosts workshops to disseminate research findings. Maintains a specialized library, open to the public, for research and study. Has developed a "step-by-step defensively-oriented route to disarmament."

Major Publications: The Institute has published numerous reports on the arms race, the U.S.–Soviet military balance, arms control negotiations and policies, the nuclear weapons freeze, and long-term strategies for peace. Publishes the *Arms Control Reporter*, a monthly looseleaf journal of worldwide arms control and disarmament developments. A national newsletter, *Defense and Disarmament News*, will begin publication in April 1985.

Institute for Policy Studies, 1901 Que Street, NW, Washington, DC 20009. The Institute for Policy Studies is a center for "research, education and social invention." It sponsors analysis of U.S. policy and proposes alternative strategies. Programs focus on national security and international policy, international economics and human rights, domestic reconstruction, and knowledge and politics.

Principal Activities: Operates a variety of educational programs designed to review present policy and consider alternative solutions. Its Transnational Institute (in Amsterdam) is dedicated to the examination of issues on the militarization of societies and worldwide insecurity.

Major Publications: Refer to the *IPS Index of Published Studies* for specific titles on arms control and disarmament.

Interchurch Peace Council (Interkerkelijk Vredesberaad) (IKV), P.O. Box 18747, 2502 ES The Hague, The Netherlands. This is one of the largest European peace movement organizations, consisting of representatives of all major churches in the Netherlands. Its aim is to contribute to a worldwide process of nuclear disarmament by removing, as a first step, all nuclear weapons from Dutch soil. The organization declares that it is neither "neutralist," nor "pacifist," nor "anti-American," but rather dedicated to peace.

Principal Activities: In 1977, the IKV launched a long-term campaign against nuclear weapons under the slogan "Help rid the world of nuclear weapons; let it begin in the Netherlands." It has since pursued this goal with determination, opposing the deployment of NATO cruise missiles on Dutch soil, and collaborating with U.S. and European disarmament groups favoring a bilateral nuclear freeze.

The International Institute for Strategic Studies, 23 Tavistock Street, London, WC2E 7NQ. The Institute is an independent center for research, information and debate on the problems of security, conflict and conflict control, and arms and arms control in the modern world. It is independent of any government or political or other organization. It, alone, decides what research to undertake and activities to conduct. All its financial support stems from nongovernmental sources. The organization's Governing Council consists of 27 leading scientists from some 15 countries of Europe, North America, and Asia. Membership extends to 60 countries.

Principal Activities: The Institute sponsors research, provides information for public use, and serves as a forum for discussion and debate on international security problems. Priority areas for research include arms limitation, force reductions, crisis control and confidence-building measures. Information activities are by means of several prestigious publications (see below). Discussion forums include the organization's Annual Conference, meetings and seminars on issues of current concern, and the Alastair Buchan Memorial Lecture.

Major Publications:
- *The Military Balance* (annual survey of military forces around the world)
- *Strategic Survey* (annual survey of significant security-related events)
- *Adelphi Papers* (series of monographs on the Institute's research findings)
- *Survival* (the Institute's journal — published six times annually).

International Physicians for the Prevention of Nuclear War, Inc., 225 Longwood Avenue, Room 240, Boston, MA 02115. This is a federation of physicians' organizations working for the prevention of nuclear war. There are thirty-four foreign affiliated organizations and a total membership of 105,000. The American affiliate is "Physicians for Social Responsibility."

Principal Activities: Sponsors international congresses and symposia to discuss the medical consequences of nuclear war. (Four congresses have been held thus far; the fifth is scheduled to meet in Budapest in June 1985.) Initiates and promotes research on the medical and psychological effects of nuclear war and communicates findings to world leaders. Furnishes speakers at meetings and rallies and visits primary and secondary schools to hear the thoughts of children about the nuclear arms race.

Major Publications: The Report (a quarterly newsletter); *The Update* (published periodically); and *Last Aid: The Medical Dimensions of Nuclear War*.

Lawyers Alliance for Nuclear Arms Control, 43 Charles Street, Suite 3, Boston, MA 02114. This is a national, nonprofit, nonpartisan organization of lawyers, judges, law students, and other legal and paralegal personnel committed to nuclear arms control and mutual nuclear disarmament. Organization believes that lawyers, more than any other professional group, can contribute to rational arms control as advocates for the negotiation of verifiable, mutual agreements for the reduction of nuclear armaments. Total membership is 6,000, organized in 48 chapters.

Principal Activities: Organization conducts educational programs, including symposia on key arms control issues, which bring together American and Soviet diplomats and experts. Promotes resolutions on arms control for consideration by state and local bars, and speaks out strongly in favor of verifiable and mutual agreements to halt and reverse the nuclear arms race. Sponsors "mock trials" and "mock negotiations" to draw public attention to nuclear arms control issues. A delegation of Alliance members met with their Soviet counterparts in Moscow in the summer of 1983 and again in Washington in 1984.

Major Publications: The Lawyers Alliance Newsletter (quarterly); *The Case Against the MX Missile*; *The Lawyers Alliance Annotated Bibliography*; and *Legal Issues of the "Star Wars" Defense Program*.

Medical Campaign Against Nuclear Weapons, 7 Tenison Road, Cambridge, CB1 2DG, United Kingdom. The organization consists of doctors and others in the health field who are united in the belief "that nuclear warfare must never be allowed to happen." Founded in 1980, the organization maintains branches in 48 cities throughout the United Kingdom and has a total membership of nearly 4,000. It is affiliated with "International Physicians for the Prevention of Nuclear War, Inc."

Principal Activities: The organization produces and distributes books, pamphlets, video tapes, and slides on the nuclear arms race; sponsors mobile exhibits which tour different parts of the United Kingdom; and participates in conferences and seminars which address the medical consequences of nuclear warfare. One aspect of special concern to the organization is the examination of the psychological effects in children living under the threat of nuclear weapons.

Major Publications: A journal, *Medicine and War*, is planned.

Mobilization for Survival, 853 Broadway, New York, NY 10003. Mobilization for Survival is a coalition of local peace, disarmament, and safe energy organizations. Its goals are: zero nuclear weapons, ban nuclear power, reverse the arms race, and meet human needs. The organization promotes a wide range of protest and educational activities, from demonstrations and nonviolent civil disobedience to referenda.

Principal Activities: The Mobilization acts both as a network for local groups and as an initiator of national activities. Assists local groups in developing their organizational and other skills; initiates and promotes national actions and campaigns to futher the organization's four goals; and provides a forum for local affiliates to participate in national issues and activities.

Major Publications: The Mobilizer, a quarterly publication used to communicate with coalition members. In addition, street leaflets, research and educational pamphlets, and organizing materials.

Nuclear Weapons Freeze Campaign, 3195 South Grand Blvd., St. Louis, MO 63118. The campaign aims at raising American consciousness about the threat of atomic war. Goal is to have U.S. and Soviet leaders halt further nuclear weapons development, production and deployment. Additionally, organization favors cutoff in all new U.S. weapons testing, if the Soviet Union promises the same; and the withdrawal of U.S. cruise and Pershing II missiles from Europe, if accompanied by a substantial Soviet reduction in intermediate range ballistic missiles targeted on Europe. Maintains nation-wide membership with chapters in all states and in hundreds of communities.

Principal Activities: Past activities have focused on "nonbinding" nuclear freeze resolutions endorsed by millions of voters. Present strategy is to pressure Congress to cut off all funds for testing and deployment of nuclear weapons, provided the Soviet Union halts all similar activities.

Major Publications: The Freeze Focus (monthly newsletter). Additional materials include a series of fact sheets entitled *The Freeze,* strategy papers, information packets, and briefing books.

Peace Development Fund, 274 North Pleasant Street, Amherst, MA 01004. The Peace Development Fund is a nonprofit, publicly supported foundation created to promote world peace and to aid the development of projects which educate the public about disarmament, global demilitarization, and the peaceful resolution of international conflict.

Principal Activities: Funds hundreds of diverse projects all across the country (the size of grants is small, however). Typical recent grants have included the distribution of films publicizing the effects of nuclear war; funding children's letter-writing campaigns for nuclear disarmament; organizing citizens' opposition to various nuclear facilities; and supporting regional organizing conferences of peace groups.

Major Publications: Peace Developments (quarterly newsletter).

Peace Links, 723½ 8th Street, SE, Washington, DC 20003. Peace Links is a nonprofit, nonpartisan organization which seeks to awaken women to the nuclear danger and to encourage them to become involved in lessening the nuclear threat. The organization's full name designation is "Peace Links, Women Against Nuclear War."

Principal Activities: Sponsors a great variety of activities (letter writing campaigns, club meetings, peace panels, coffee parties, etc.) "so women can work together in finding ways to end the nuclear threat." Organizes "Peace Day," on the first Sunday in October, as a day of public recognition of the desire for continued peace.

Major Publications: Disseminates materials designed to assist organizers in establishing Peace Links at the local level: *Coffee Party Packet, Peace Panel Packet, Government Process Packet,* and *Local Research Questionnaire.*

Physicians for Social Responsibility, 639 Massachusetts Avenue, Cambridge, MA 02139. This is a national, nonprofit organization of physicians, dentists and medical students dedicated to professional and public education on the medical hazards of nuclear war. Total membership is approximately 30,000.

Principal Activities: Organization works to educate the general public and government leaders on the health implications of nuclear weapons and the threat of nuclear war. Utilizes local chapters and other affiliated organizations to lobby for specific arms control issues (i.e., for the bilateral freeze, for a Comprehensive Test Ban Treaty, and against the production and emplacement of first strike weapons). Promotes the introduction of courses in medical schools on the effects of nuclear weapons. Maintains a Washington office which serves as a liaison with the Congress and the Administration. Sponsors symposia on the medical consequences of nuclear war. Local chapters serve as resource centers for speakers and materials.

Major Publications: Quarterly Newsletter. Has available also for sale or rent a large number of videocassettes, slides, and films, including "The Last Epidemic: The Medical Consequences of Nuclear Weapons and Nuclear War," a highly acclaimed film.

Ploughshares Fund, Fort Mason, San Francisco, CA 94123. Ploughshares is a public charitable foundation specifically directed to fund organizations and individuals whose work is focused on arms control. The organization supports a foreign policy founded on global collaboration and emphasizes U.S.–Soviet cooperation as the cornerstone of world security.

Principal Activities: Ploughshares funds projects which, in the opinion of its Board of Directors, strengthen world security and help prevent nuclear war. Approximately 100 projects have been funded since the Fund's establishment in 1981. Notable recent grants have included support of a major study on verification of arms control agreements, the establishment of an 800-number to take calls from citizens concerned about the danger of nuclear war; and Congressional lobbying activities in support of a Bilateral Nuclear Freeze.

Professionals' Coalition, 1346 Connecticut Ave. NW, Suite 1117, Washington, DC 20036. This is a coalition of three arms control organizations whose aim is to enact realistic and substantial arms control legislation. The Coalition is working for a mutually verifiable bilateral weapons freeze, for a comprehensive nuclear test ban treaty, against the MX, and against an arms race in outer space. Its activities are exclusively on Capitol Hill.

Major publications: The Professional (a periodical) and *Citizen Lobbyist Skills Manual*.

Rand Corporation, 1700 Main Street, Santa Monica, CA 90406. The Rand Corporation is a private, nonprofit institution engaged in research and analysis of matters affecting national security and the public welfare. The Corporation conducts its own work with support from federal, state, and local governments and from foundations and other private philanthropic sources. Because of its wide range of interests, research on arms control issues represent only a small segment of RAND's program.

Major Publications (on arms control): Listed in annotated RAND bibliography, entitled *Selected RAND Publications—Arms Control*, June 1983.

Riverside Church Disarmament Program, 490 Riverside Drive, New York, NY 10027. The Riverside Church is in the forefront of the disarmament movement. It publishes educational materials on the nuclear arms race, nuclear war, and disarmament; provides speakers to church groups and civic and professional associations; sponsors "Vigils for Peace"; and hosts seminars attended by leading authorities in the field.

Major Publications: The Arms Race and Us and *Disarming Notes*, a bimonthly newsletter.

The Rockefeller Foundation, 1133 Avenue of the Americas, New York, NY 10036. The Rockefeller Foundation is a philanthropic organization endowed by John D. Rockefeller for the purpose of promoting "the well-being of mankind throughout the world." It seeks to identify and attack at their source the underlying causes of human suffering and need. Programs are carried out directly by the Foundation; through grants to universities, research institutes, and other organizations conducting work within the scope of the Foundation's programs; through a program of fellowship awards; and through the general dissemination of knowledge.

Principal Activities (only arms control/disarmament activities are listed): The Foundation provides funding for independent research, policy analysis, and training in the field of international security, with emphasis on U.S.–Soviet relations. Recent grants have been for the purpose of informing the American public about Soviet policies and actions, especially with regard to prospects for nuclear arms control.

SANE, 711 G Street, SE, Washington, DC 20003. SANE (The Committee for a Sane Nuclear Policy) is a citizens' organization dedicated to preventing war and ending the "insane buildup of arms" by both the United States and the Soviet Union. Its membership exceeds 100,000.

Principal Activities: Lobbies with the Congress and activates citizens groups in support of specific arms control causes (e.g. halting production of MX missiles; for a moratorium on ASAT testing; opposing chemical weapons production). Prepares and distributes educational materials to schools, religious groups, and civic organizations. Maintains an arms control computer network which links the offices and activities of seven national organizations into a single-movement-wide network. Sponsors "Consider the Alternatives," a weekly radio broadcast aired over 140 stations. Utilized a Political Action Committee (SANE PAC), during the 1984 national elections, to support candidates favoring arms reductions.

Major Publications: Sane World (a monthly newsletter) and *Help Wanted*. Also numerous brochures, flyers, and reading packets.

The Stanley Foundation, 420 E. Third Street, Muscatine, Iowa 52761. The Stanley Foundation works toward the goal of "a secure peace with freedom and justice" by encouraging study, research and discussion of international issues. A private organization, all its activities are internally planned, funded, and administered. Conference attendance is by invitation only.

Principal Activities: The Foundation hosts annually several conferences and meetings dedicated to a reevaluation of U.S. foreign policy. Arms control and disarmament are key issues discussed, especially at the "Strategy for Peace Conference." Additionally, the Foundation sponsors a public radio series entitled "Common Ground," publishes papers addressing international issues, and edits the *World Press Review*, a monthly periodical which excerpts and reports materials from the foreign press.

Major Publications: World Press Review (monthly) and miscellaneous conference reports and papers.

Stockholm International Peace Research Institute (SIPRI), Bergshamra, S-171 73 Solna, Sweden. SIPRI is an independent institute for research into problems of peace and conflict, with particular attention to issues of arms control and disarmament. It was founded by the Swedish Parliament in July 1966 to commemorate Sweden's 150 years of unbroken peace.

Although funded by the Swedish Parliament, SIPRI is independent of the Swedish government. Its policies and operations are the responsibility of an international governing board and its staff is recruited from different geographic regions and economic systems. Day-to-day operations are under a Director, assisted by a Scientific Council.

Principal Activities: SIPRI deals exclusively with issues of armaments and disarmament (i.e., military expenditures, military deployments and arms trade; military technology; and specific arms control and disarmament issues). Research and publication of findings constitute the principal activity, supported by an outstanding library (not open to the general public) and an in-depth data base for certain subjects of continuing interest.

Major Publications: Principal publication is the *Annual Yearbook of World Armaments and Disarmament*. Other SIPRI publications (about 50 books and 20 research reports) are distributed by Taylor and Francis Ltd., New York and London.

Student/Teacher Organization to Prevent Nuclear War (STOP), 636 Beacon Street, Boston, MA 02215. STOP Nuclear War is an educational organization of high school students and teachers committed to reducing the threat of nuclear war. Its goals are to educate students, teachers, and the community about the nuclear arms race; to demonstrate that educated, organized groups can make a meaningful contribution to the efforts to prevent nuclear war; and to effect changes which will increase governments' receptivity to security strategies not based on nuclear weapons.

Principal Activities: Sponsors activities to educate members and their communities about the nuclear arms race and of efforts to reverse it. Recent activities have included: media presentations on the arms race; letter writing campaigns to local newspapers; educational displays in libraries and other public places; debates; teach-ins; and conferences.

Major Publications: Publishes regularly *STOP NEWS* to guide local chapters. Also: *STOP Nuclear War: First Steps*; and *It's Your Future: Stop Nuclear War*.

Union of Concerned Scientists, 26 Church Street, Cambridge, MA 02238. The Union of Concerned Scientists is a national organization of scientists and citizens concerned about the impact of advanced technology on society. Its primary goals are a safe, sensible course for America's energy program and a world free from the threat of nuclear war. The organization is supported financially by donations from more than 100,000 individuals, nationwide.

Principal Activities: The Union conducts educational activities, public interest litigation and legislative lobbying in the areas of nuclear power safety, national energy policy, and nuclear arms control. These activities are supported by independent technical research and analysis conducted by the organization's professional scientists and engineers. Recent activities in the arms control area have included:

- Teach-ins at numerous universities on the dangers of the nuclear arms race;
- Declaration on the Nuclear Arms Race;
- Convocations on Nuclear War; and
- Advocacy of American adoption of a policy of No First Use of nuclear weapons.

Major Publications: Nucleus (newsletter); other publications such as: *Beyond the Freeze*; *Choices*; and *No First Use*.

United Campuses to Prevent Nuclear War (UCAM), 1346 Connecticut Avenue, NW, Suite 706, Washington, DC 20036. This is a U.S.–Canadian network of university students, faculty and staff "working to end the nuclear arms race." The organization's role is that of a catalyst, providing campuses with direction and the means for influencing government arms policy. Goals are: the achievement of major reductions in U.S. and Soviet nuclear weapons; and the end of the superpowers' arms race. Maintains chapters in over 60 campuses across the United States and Canada.

Principal Activities: Sponsors nationwide convocations on the dangers of nuclear war. Conducts educational programs on campuses consisting of teach-ins, conferences and debates, films, slide shows, and literature distribution. Lobbies on specific arms control issues (*for* a bilateral nuclear freeze; *against* the MX).

Major Publications: UCAM Network News (monthly newsletter); *Summary of Nuclear War Syllabi; What About the Russians; Nuclear War: The Responsibility of the University; Who Decides? A Citizens Guide to Government Decision-Making on Nuclear War;* and *Organizing the Campuses to Prevent Nuclear War.*

United Nations Institute for Disarmament Research, Palais des Nations, Geneva. The Institute was established in 1980 as an autonomous organization within the framework of the United Nations. It undertakes independent research on disarmament and related security issues and works in close relationship with the U.N. Department of Disarmament Affairs. The Institute is financed by voluntary contributions from governments, nongovernment organizations, foundations, and individuals.

Women's Action for Nuclear Disarmament, Inc. (WAND), P.O. Box 153, New Town Branch, Boston, MA 02258. This is a national membership organization of more than 100 affiliate groups in 35 states. Its goal is to "educate and empower individuals to become involved in work to halt the nuclear arms race."

Principal Activities: WAND sponsors activities to increase national awareness (primarily among women) on the issues of war and peace. It organizes grassroots lobbying campaigns, supports political candidates opposed to the nuclear arms race, and participates in Mother's Day celebrations with a pro-peace theme. WAND maintains also an "Education Fund" whose primary purpose is to provide information and educational materials about nuclear disarmament. Fund activities include also speaker training and voter registration and the distribution of radio and TV spots, featuring famous American entertainers in messages supporting arms control.

Major Publications: The *WAND Bulletin* (a quarterly newsletter).

World Federalist Association (WFA), 418 7th Street, SE, Washington, DC 20003. This is a nonprofit, educational association and one of the oldest peace groups in the country. Its goal is the abolition of war between nations and the creation of a structured and just world community. WFA is a member of the World Association of World Federalists headquartered in Amsterdam, the Netherlands. U.S. membership is approximately 10,000 organized in some 90 local groups.

Principal Activities: WFA is active with numerous other national coalitions supporting peace, disarmament, and world order. Its support of these activites is in the form of lobbying, issuance of action alerts, and staff participation. The organization has been in the forefront of the movement to revive the spirit of the McCloy-Zorin Agreement of 1961, as the foundation for future negotiations toward general disarmament.

World Policy Institute, 777 United Nations Plaza, New York, NY 10017. The purpose of the World Policy Institute is to develop and implement practical proposals for the peaceful resolution of global conflicts; for building an equitable and sustainable world economy; and the protection of human rights and global ecology. Formerly the Institute for World Order, the organization changed its name in 1982 to reflect an increased emphasis on scholarly research.

Principal Activities: Sponsors research on a large number of arms control and disarmament issues. Research is performed in-house by Institute staff or specialists working under the umbrella of the "Security Project." Hosts conferences and training sessions, publishes research findings, and lobbies with legislators and public officials on issues promoting the organization's objectives.

Major Publications: World Policy Forum (twice each year); the *World Policy Journal*, a new quarterly launched in November 1983; and *Alternatives*, a quarterly journal copublished with the Centre for the Study of Developing Societies in New Delhi.

Part III
Reference Data

Acronyms

ABM	Antiballistic missile
ACDA	U.S. Arms Control and Disarmament Agency
ACIS	Arms control impact statement
ALCM	Air-launched cruise missile
ASAT	Antisatellite (system/weapon)
ASW	Antisubmarine warfare/weapon
AWACS	Airborne warning and control system
BMD	Ballistic missile defense
BMEWS	Ballistic missile early warning system
BWC	Biological weapons convention
CBM	Confidence-building measures
CBR	Chemical, biological, and radiological (weapons)
CCCI	Command, control, communications and intelligence
CD	Conference on Disarmament
CEP	Circular error probable
CM	Cruise missile
CSCE	Conference on Security and Cooperation in Europe
CTBT	Comprehensive Test Ban Treaty
CW	Chemical warfare/weapon
DC	Disarmament Commission
DOD	Department of Defense
DU	Depleted uranium
EURATOM	European Atomic Energy Agency
FBMS	Fleet ballistic missile system
FBS	Forward-based systems
FOBS	Fractional orbital bombardment system
GLCM	Ground-launched cruise missile
GZ	Ground Zero
HEU	Highly enriched uranium
HOB	Height of burst

IAEA	International Atomic Energy Agency
ICBM	Intercontinental ballistic missile
INF	Intermediate-range nuclear forces
IR	Infrared
IRBM	Intermediate range ballistic missile
KT	Kiloton
LRTNF	Long-range theater nuclear forces
MAD	Mutual assured destruction
MBFR	Mutual and balanced force reductions
MDW	Mass destruction weapons
MIRV	Multiple, independently-targeted reentry vehicle
MRV	Multiple reentry vehicle
MT	Megaton
MX	Missile experimental
NATO	North Atlantic Treaty Organization
NNPA	Nuclear Nonproliferation Act
NNWS	Nonnuclear weapon states
NPT	Nuclear Non-Proliferation Treaty
NSC	National Security Council
NTM	National technical means (of verification)
NWFZ	Nuclear weapons free zone
OAS	Organization of American states
OPANAL	Agency for the Prohibition of Nuclear Weapons in Latin America
OTH	Over-the-horizon
PNE	Peaceful nuclear explosion
PSI	Pounds per square inch
PTBT	Partial Test Ban Treaty
R&D	Research and development
REM	Roentgen equivalent man
RES	Resolution
RV	Reentry vehicle
RW	Radiological weapons
SAC	Strategic Air Command
SALT	Strategic Arms Limitation Talks
SAM	Surface-to-air-missile
SCC	Standing Consultative Commission
SIOP	Single, integrated, operational plan
SLBM	Submarine-launched ballistic missile
SLCM	Sea-launched cruise missile
SRF	Strategic rocket forces
SSBN	Submarine, ballistic nuclear
SSN	Submarine, nuclear-powered

SSOD	Special Session on Disarmament
START	Strategic Arms Reduction Talks
TNF	Theater nuclear forces
TNW	Theater nuclear war
TTBT	Threshold Test Ban Treaty
WP	Warsaw Pact

Chronology of Key Arms Control Events

June 17, 1925	Geneva Convention is signed.
February 8, 1928	Geneva Convention enters force.
August 6 and 11, 1945	U.S. forces strike Hiroshima and Nagasaki with nuclear weapons.
June 14, 1946	U.S. representative to the U.N. Atomic Energy Commission, Bernard Baruch, presents plan calling for placing all atomic resources of the world under an international authority (the Baruch Plan). Plan is rejected five days later by the Soviet Union.
April 1949	NATO is formed. The United States pledges to use nuclear weapons in defense of Europe.
September 1949	President Truman announces the detonation of a nuclear device by the Soviet Union. Shortly thereafter he orders U.S. development of the hydrogen bomb.
1952	The United States explodes a hydrogen device. A year later the Soviet Union conducts a similar test.
1952	The United Kingdom tests an atomic bomb and thus becomes the world's third nuclear power.
1952	The U.N. Disarmament Commission is established.
December 8, 1953	President Eisenhower makes his Atoms-for-Peace proposal before the U.N. General Assembly.
March 1954	The United States announces a policy of "massive retaliation" as a basic strategy for deterring Soviet aggression.

June 11, 1954	France and the United Kingdom call for "balanced arms reductions leading to complete disarmament." Proposal is supported by the U.S. Government.
1954	The United States and the Soviet Union begin developing ballistic missile systems.
1955	President Eisenhower presents his "Open Skies" proposal. Would allow U.S. and Soviet reconnaissance flights over each other's territory as a confidence-building measure while arms reductions are being negotiated.
May 1955	Negotiations designed to ban nuclear testing start in the U.N. Disarmament Commission.
1956	United States begins reconnaissance flights over the Soviet Union using the U-2 plane.
July 29, 1957	The International Atomic Energy Agency (IAEA) comes into being in Vienna, Austria. Its objective is to "accelerate and enlarge the contribution of atomic energy to peace, health and prosperity."
October 4, 1957	The Soviet Union launches its first man-made satellite "Sputnik." Alarmed, the United States begins development of several strategic programs.
1958	The United States begins flight-testing its Atlas ICBM system; deploys intermediate-range Thor and Jupiter missiles in Europe.
1959	A "missile gap" is reported by the Gaither Committee and is debated during the 1960 presidential campaign.
October 15, 1959	The Conference on Antarctica opens in Washington with eleven nations participating.
December 1, 1959	Antarctic Treaty is opened for signature.
March 1960	Ten-nation Disarmament Conference is convened in Geneva. The Soviet Union proposes "general and complete disarmament."
1960	France conducts its first nuclear test in the Sahara, thus becoming the world's fourth nuclear power.
August 10, 1960	U.S. Senate advises ratification of the Antarctic Treaty.
September 22, 1960	President Eisenhower proposes to the U.N. General Assembly that the principles of the Antarctic Treaty be applied also to outer space.

March 1961	The United States begins an expansion of its nuclear strategic forces to close the "missile gap."
June 23, 1961	Antarctic Treaty enters force.
September 25, 1961	President Kennedy presents to the U.N. General Assembly a program for "general and complete disarmament in a peaceful world."
1961	The U.N. General Assembly calls upon all nuclear powers to conclude a Non-Proliferation Treaty, as a means of controlling the transfer of nuclear technology to nonnuclear states.
1962	Eighteen-nation Disarmament Committee (ENDC) is established (this is the predecessor organization of the Conference on Disarmament).
1962	The United States establishes the Arms Control and Disarmament Agency (ACDA) to deal with issues of arms control and disarmament.
1962	The United States abandons its strategy of "massive retaliation." Adopts a strategy of "flexible response" for dealing with the Soviet Union.
October 1962	The Cuban missile crisis. Brings the world to the brink of nuclear disaster. Event gives a strong impetus to arms control and the need for accommodation between the two major nuclear powers.
April 29, 1963	The presidents of several Latin American nations announce their willingness to sign an agreement banning nuclear weapons from their continent.
June 20, 1963	The United States and the Soviet Union sign the "Hot Line" Agreement.
August 5, 1963	The Limited Test Ban Treaty is signed in Moscow. It bans nuclear testing in the atmosphere, in outer space, or under water.
September 24, 1963	The U.S. Senate advises ratification of the Limited Test Ban Treaty.
October 10, 1963	The Limited Test Ban Treaty enters force.
October 17, 1963	The U.N. General Assembly adopts a resolution welcoming U.S. and Soviet declarations against the placement of nuclear weapons in outer space.
1964	China tests an atomic bomb, thus becoming the world's fifth nuclear power.

1966	The Soviet Union begins deployment of an ABM defense system around Moscow.
January 27, 1967	The Outer Space Treaty is signed. Bans the placement of nuclear weapons in Earth orbit or on celestial bodies.
February 14, 1967	The treaty prohibiting nuclear weapons in Latin America is signed in Tlatelolco.
April 25, 1967	The U.S. Senate advises ratification of the Outer Space Treaty.
August 24, 1967	The United States and the Soviet Union agree on the key provisions of a Nuclear Non-Proliferation Treaty.
September 18, 1967	President Johnson announces decision to build a "thin" ABM system to guard against an anticipated Chinese ICBM threat in the 1970s and beyond.
October 10, 1967	The Outer Space Treaty enters force.
December 5, 1967	The U.N. General Assembly endorses the Latin America Nuclear Free Zone Treaty.
December 18, 1967	The U.N. General Assembly establishes a Committee to study ways of preserving the seabed for peaceful purposes.
April 1, 1968	The United States signs Protocol II to the Latin America Nuclear Free Zone Treaty.
July 1, 1968	The Nuclear Non-Proliferation Treaty is signed in Washington, Moscow, and London.
August 1968	The United States successfully test-fires its first MIRVed warhead.
August 1968	Soviet forces invade Czechoslovakia, delaying U.S. Senate ratification of the Nuclear Non-Proliferation Treaty.
March 13, 1969	The U.S. Senate advises ratification of the Nuclear Non-Proliferation Treaty.
March 18, 1969	The Soviet Union proposes demilitarizing the seabed beyond a 12-mile limit.
May 22, 1969	The United States proposes a treaty prohibiting the emplacement of nuclear weapons on the seabed and the ocean floor.
November 17, 1969	SALT talks begin in Helsinki.
November 25, 1969	The United States renounces unilaterally and unconditionally all methods of biological warfare.
November 25, 1969	President Nixon resubmits the Geneva Proto-

	col to the Senate for ratification. (Had been previously considered by the Senate but withdrawn by President Truman in 1948.)
February 14, 1970	The United States extends its November 25, 1969 pledge regarding biological warfare also to all toxins.
March 5, 1970	The Nuclear Non-Proliferation Treaty enters force.
August 5, 1970	The United States and Soviet Union submit separate but identical texts for a U.N. convention outlawing the development, production, and stockpiling of biological and toxin weapons.
December 7, 1970	The U.N. General Assembly approves the draft Seabed Arms Control Treaty.
February 11, 1971	The Seabed Arms Control Treaty is signed at U.N. Headquarters.
April 19, 1971	The U.S. Senate advises ratification of Protocol II to the Latin America Treaty.
September 30, 1971	The United States and Soviet Union sign in Washington the "Hot Line" Improvement and Modernization Agreement and an Agreement on Measures to Reduce the Risk of Outbreak of Nuclear War.
February 15, 1972	The U.S. Senate advises ratification of the Seabed Arms Control Treaty.
April 10, 1972	The Biological Weapons Convention is signed in Washington, Moscow and London.
May 18, 1972	The Seabed Arms Control Treaty enters force.
May 26, 1972	President Nixon and Soviet leader Brezhnev sign the SALT I agreement in Moscow. Consists of the ABM Treaty and an Interim Agreement on the Limitation of Strategic Offensive Arms.
July 1972	The United States renounces the use of climate modification techniques for hostile purposes.
September 30, 1972	The U.S. Senate advises ratification of the SALT I agreement.
October 3, 1972	SALT I enters force.
December 21, 1972	The United States and the Soviet Union sign in Geneva a Memorandum of Understanding for the Establishment of the Standing Consultative Commission.
June 22, 1973	The United States and Soviet Union sign in

	Washington the Agreement for the Prevention of Nuclear War.
1973	The MBFR nonnuclear forces talks start in Vienna between NATO and the Warsaw Pact.
1973	The United States and Soviet Union launch the SALT II talks designed to further limit offensive nuclear arms.
1974	India detonates a nuclear device, thus becoming the world's sixth nuclear power.
July 3, 1974	Protocol to the ABM Treaty is signed in Moscow. Limits U.S. and Soviet ABM deployments to one site each.
July 3, 1974	The U.S. and Soviet Union sign the Threshold Test Ban Treaty limiting underground nuclear tests to no more than 150 KT.
November 24, 1974	President Ford and Secretary-General Brezhnev meet in Vladivostok and agree on a framework for future limitations in strategic offensive weapons.
December 16, 1974	The U.S. Senate advises ratification of the Biological Weapons Convention.
January 22, 1975	The U.S. ratifies the Geneva Protocol of 1925.
March 26, 1975	The Biological Weapons Convention enters force.
May 1975	The First Review Conference on the Nuclear Non-Proliferation Treaty meets in Geneva.
August 1975	The U.S. and Soviet Union table parallel and identical draft texts for a convention on the prohibition of military and other hostile uses of the environment.
May 28, 1976	The United States and Soviet Union sign the Treaty on the Limitation of Underground Nuclear Explosions for Peaceful Purposes.
December 10, 1976	The U.N. General Assembly endorses the U.S. and Soviet framework for an Environmental Convention.
1977	The Soviet Union begins deployment in Eastern Europe of the SS-20 intermediate range missile.
1977	President Carter offers proposal calling for deep reductions in the numbers of strategic weapons agreed to at Vladivostok.
May 18, 1977	The Environmental Modification Convention is signed.

May 26, 1977	The United States signs Protocol I to the Latin American Nuclear Free Zone Treaty (also called the Treaty of Tlatelolco).
November 18, 1977	The United States signs agreement with the IAEA permitting the latter organization to apply its safeguard controls to all U.S. nuclear facilities, except those with "direct" national security significance.
1977	President Carter cancels the B-1 bomber, but decides to equip the B-52 bomber fleet with long-range cruise missiles.
1978	Bilateral negotiations between the United States and the Soviet Union begin in Geneva. Are designed to limit the growth of anti-satellite weapons.
March 10, 1978	President Carter signs the Non-Proliferation Act.
May to July, 1978	The First Special Session of the U.N. General Assembly devoted exclusively to disarmament meets in New York.
June 18, 1979	SALT II, the Treaty on the Limitation of Strategic Offensive Arms, is signed in Vienna by President Carter and Soviet Secretary-General Brezhnev.
November 28, 1979	The U.S. Senate advises ratification of the Environmental Modification Convention.
December 12, 1979	NATO Foreign Ministers approve a framework for modernization of the alliance's theater nuclear forces and for negotiations with the Soviets to limit nuclear weapons in Europe. (the "Dual Track Decision").
1979	President Carter announces plans to construct a multiple protective shelter system (the "Race Track") as a means of protecting the proposed MX ICBM force.
January 3, 1980	President Carter requests that Senate delay consideration of the SALT II Treaty in light of the Soviet invasion of Afghanistan.
August-September, 1980	The Second Review Conference on the Nuclear Non-Proliferation Treaty meets in Geneva.
October 19, 1980	Candidate Reagan describes SALT II as "basically flawed" because it does not reduce armaments.

1981	The Reagan Administration begins a major defense build-up.
March 1981	The Nuclear Weapons Freeze Campaign is launched by a group of arms control activists.
April 10, 1981	The Convention on Inhumane Weapons is opened for signature at U.N. Headquarters.
November 18, 1981	President Reagan announces his "zero option" position for the upcoming Geneva talks on limiting intermediate nuclear forces (INF) in Europe.
November 30, 1981	U.S.–Soviet INF talks begin in Geneva.
May 9, 1982	At Eureka College, IL, President Reagan announces his plan for strategic arms control. Proposes phased reductions in ballistic missiles. Talks to be known as START.
June 18, 1982	Soviet leaders describe President Reagan's START proposal as "a step in the right direction," but also criticize it as "absolutely unilateral in nature."
June 7 to July 10, 1982	Second Special Session of the U.N. General Assembly devoted to disarmament.
June 10–12, 1982	Massive demonstrations in New York and several European cities call for action to halt the nuclear arms race.
June 29, 1982	START talks begin in Geneva.
June 1982	Private "Walk in the Woods" discussions between the U.S. and Soviet negotiators at the INF talks in Geneva. Formula for agreement is repudiated by the U.S. and Soviet governments.
July 1982	NATO tables new draft treaty at the MBFR talks in Vienna in an effort to revitalize the stalemated negotiations.
November 22, 1982	President Reagan in a speech to the nation announces his decision to deploy 100 MX missiles in a closely spaced or "Dense Pack" basing scheme. Urges the Soviet Union to negotiate significant strategic arms reductions.
December 1982	Soviet media denounce the proposed "Dense Pack" deployment as a violation of SALT I and II agreements.
December 21, 1982	Soviet leader Yuri Andropov proposes the creation of a nuclear-free zone in Europe.

January 21, 1983	The Pershing II missile completes its first successful test flight.
March 23, 1983	President Reagan announces his Strategic Defense Initiative (SDI) proposal. ("Star Wars" speech).
April 6, 1983	The Scowcroft Commission delivers its report to the President. Key elements of the report are incorporated into the U.S. START position.
May 4, 1983	The House of Representatives by a vote of 278–149 passes a resolution calling for negotiations for a mutual and verifiable freeze on and reductions in nuclear forces.
August 1983	Soviets submit draft treaty to the U.N. General Assembly calling for the elimination of existing ASAT systems and a ban on the development of new ASATs. Announce unilateral moratorium.
October 22, 1983	More than one million West Germans and over 200,000 Londoners demonstrate to protest the deployment of Pershing IIs and cruise missiles in their countries. Smaller demonstrations occur in other European cities.
October 31, 1983	The British House of Commons supports the deployment of cruise missiles on its territory. Action is followed immediately by U.S. delivery of first medium-range nuclear missiles to Greenham Common Air Base.
November 16, 1983	The Italian Chamber of Deputies approves the deployment of cruise missiles on Italian soil. Is followed a week later by a similar vote in the German Bundestag.
November 23, 1983	The first Pershing II missiles arrive in the Federal Republic of Germany.
November 23, 1983	The Soviets walk out of the Geneva INF talks in protest of U.S. deployment of Pershing II and cruise missiles in Western Europe.
December 8, 1983	The Soviets suspend also the START negotiations.
December 13, 1983	Secretary of Defense Caspar W. Weinberger reports that the total Soviet deployment of the SS-20 missile system has reached 369.
January 16, 1984	The Conference on Confidence and Security Building of the European Disarmament Conference starts in Stockholm.

January 21, 1984	The U.S. Air Force conducts the first successful test of a missile designed to destroy a satellite in orbit.
January 23, 1984	President Reagan sends a report to the Congress accusing the Soviet Union of serious arms control violations. Counter-charges of U.S. violations are made in Moscow.
March 1984	Reports from the Iran-Iraqi front suggest that Iraq has used poison gas.
April 18, 1984	Vice-President Bush unveils before the Conference on Disarmament in Geneva a draft treaty banning chemical weapons.
May 14, 1984	The Soviet Union announces deployment of additional nuclear missiles in Eastern Germany to counter the continuing build-up in Western Europe of U.S. Pershing II and cruise missiles.
May 18, 1984	The House of Representatives votes to deny funds for the production of chemical weapons.
June 11, 1984	Soviet President Chernenko calls on the U.S. to negotiate a ban on the use of ASAT weapons.
June 29, 1984	The United States responds to Chernenko's call but proposes broader agenda, including resumption of the suspended INF and START talks.
July 1, 1984	The Soviet Government rejects as "totally unsatisfactory" the U.S. position (above), thus frustrating the start of negotiations.
July 18, 1984	The United States and Soviet Union agree to upgrade the communications capabilities of the "Hot Line."
October 10 and 11, 1984	The United States and Soviet Union accuse each other of arms control violations.
November 13, 1984	The United States conducts its first test flight of an ASAT warhead over Vandenberg Air Force Base, CA.
December 3, 1984	Soviet President Chernenko says that a U.S. pledge not to "use first" nuclear weapons could lead to a summit meeting with President Reagan.
January 7 and 8, 1985	Secretary of State George P. Shultz and his Soviet counterpart Andrei A. Gromyko meet in Geneva and agree to begin arms control negotiations in three areas: space, strategic weapons, and intermediate range weapons.

Arms Control Related Legislation, 98th Congress

U.S. Senate

Key Votes:

- Approved amendment to the FY 1985 Defense Authorization Bill prohibiting ASAT testing until the President certifies that several conditions have been met, including demonstration that the United States is attempting to negotiate in good faith arms limitations in this area (July 12, 1984).

- Urged the President to seek Senate ratification of the Threshold Test Ban Treaty and of the Treaty on Underground Nuclear Explosions for Peaceful Purposes (June 20, 1984).

- Defeated the Nuclear Freeze proposal twice: in October 31, 1982 and again in October 5, 1984. The latter was in the form of an amendment to the Debt Limit Increase Bill.

Principal Resolutions Considered:

- *S.J. RES. 28* (introduced by Senator Tsongas, February 3, 1983) July 14, 1983)
  Resolution called upon the President to seek agreement with the Soviet Union on a moratorium on the testing in space of antisatellite weapons, to be followed by a mutual and verifiable ban on the testing, production, deployment, and use of antisatellite weapons.

- *S,J, RES. 28* (introduced by Senator Tsongas on February 3, 1983) Resolution called upon the President to resume immediately bilateral talks with the Soviet Union for the purpose of negotiating a treaty which would prohibit the testing, production, deployment, or use of space-based, air-based, or ground-based weapons designed to damage, destroy, or interfere with the functioning of spacecraft of any nation.

- *S.J. RES. 2* (introduced by Senator Kennedy with 33 co-sponsors, January 26, 1983)
  Resolution called for an immediate and complete halt to the nuclear arms race and a mutual verifiable freeze giving special attention to destabilizing weapons.

- *S. RES. 57* (introduced by Senator Cohen with 44 co-sponsors, February 3, 1983)
  Resolution expressed the sense of the Senate that the governments of the United States and the Soviet Union adhere to the principle of a guaranteed strategic build-down of nuclear forces, subject to agreed procedures of verification and compliance.

- *S. RES 83* (introduced by Senator Hart, March 8, 1983)
  Resolution urged the United States and the Soviet Union to expand their negotiations in Geneva to consider ways to prevent the use of nuclear weapons and to reduce the danger of war through accident or miscalculation.

- *S. RES. 159* (introduced by Senator Levin with 10 co-sponsors, June 16, 1983)
  Resolution expressed the sense of the Senate that the United States should propose a mutual pause in flight tests of new MIRVed ICBMS and seek an arms control agreement in the START talks incorporating the recommendations of the Scowcroft Commission.

- *S. CON. RES. 46* (introduced by Senator Dole with 7 co-sponsors, June 16, 1983)
  Resolution urged the President to propose to the government of the Soviet Union: a mutual and verifiable freeze of nuclear forces in such a manner that the United States is not limited to nuclear forces inferior to those of the Soviet Union; and practical measures to reduce the danger of nuclear war by accident or miscalculation.

- *S. CON. RES. 111* (introduced by Senator Mathias with 11 co-sponsors, May 3, 1984)
  Resolution expressed the sense of the Senate regarding a mutual and verifiable moratorium on any further deployment of sea-launched cruise missiles equipped with nuclear warheads.

U.S. House of Representatives

Key Votes:

- Approved Nuclear Freeze Resolution (May 4, 1983).
- Defeated move to initiate production of new binary chemical weapons (May 17, 1984).
- Approved delay in ASAT testing until the President has certified that the Soviet Union has conducted similar test (May 23, 1984).
- Rejected delay in Pershing II and ground-launched cruise missiles deployment in Europe (May 31, 1984).
- Approved amendment to the FY 1985 Defense Authorization Bill requiring the Congress to vote again, after April 1, 1985, before FY 1985 funds for the MX could be spent (May 31, 1984).

Principal Resolutions Considered:

- *H.J. RES. 87* (introduced by Congressman Kastenmeier, January 25, 1983)
  Resolution called on the United States to contribute actively to the goal of preventing outer space from becoming an area of military confrontation. Urged the President to enter into negotiations with the Soviet Union for a verifiable comprehensive treaty banning the testing, production, deployment and use of space-based weapons.

- *H.J. RES. 120* (introduced by Congressman Moakley with 126 co-sponsors, February 2, 1983)
  Resolution called upon the President to resume immediately bilateral talks with the Soviet Union for the purpose of negotiating a comprehensive treaty prohibiting the testing, production, deployment, or use of any space-based, air-based, or ground-based weapons system which is designed to damage, destroy, or interfere with the functioning of any spacecraft of any nation.

- *H.J. RES. 2* (introduced by Congressman Markey with 189 co-sponsors, January 3, 1983)
  Resolution called for a mutual and verifiable freeze on and reductions in nuclear weapons.

- *H. RES. 233* (introduced by Congressman Wyden, June 15, 1983)
  Resolution urged the President to enter into negotiations with the

Soviet Union to conclude a treaty providing for mutual cooperation to deal with the threat of accidental nuclear war caused by
acts of terrorism.

- *H.J. RES. 4* (introduced by Congressman Broomfield with 51 co-
  sponsors, January 3, 1983)
  Resolution called for mutual and verifiable reductions in nuclear
  arsenals. Expressed the full support of the Congress for the INF
  and START negotiations in Geneva.

- *H.J. RES. 61* (introduced by Congressman Gore with 102 co-
  sponsors, January 6, 1983)
  Resolution called on the United States and the Soviet Union to
  give first priority in the START negotiations to eliminating the fear
  of a nuclear first strike.

- *H. CON. RES. 20* (introduced by Congressman Brown, CA, with
  29 co-sponsors, January 6, 1983)
  Resolution expressed the sense of the Congress that the common
  security of all nations is threatened by the escalating arms race
  and that the danger of nuclear war requires renewed and persis-
  tent efforts to negotiate a comprehensive treaty for a staged disarmament to be verified by an international security and disarmament authority and accompanied by strengthened international
  peacekeeping and dispute resolution institutions.

Resolution Approved:
- *H.J. RES. 13* (introduced by Congressman Zablocki with 200 co-
  sponsors, January 3, 1983.) Referred to House Committee on
  Foreign Affairs where hearings were held February and March
  1983. Reported to the House, as amended, on March 14, 1983.
  Considered by the House during March and April 1983. Was
  amended and passed by the House on May 4, 1983 by a vote of
  278-149.

Key provisions:
"...consistent with the maintenance of essential equivalence in
overall nuclear capabilities at present and in the future, the Strategic Arms Reduction Talks between the United States and the
Soviet Union should have the following objectives:
(1) Pursuing the objective of negotiating an immediate, mutual,
and verifiable freeze, then pursuing the objective of negotiating

immediate, mutual, and verifiable reductions in nuclear weapons.

(2) Consistent with the above objective, giving special attention to destabilizing weapons, especially those which give either nation capabilities which confer upon it even the hypothetical advantages of a first strike.

(3) Providing for cooperative measures of verification, including provisions for onsite inspection, as appropriate, to complement National Technical Means of Verification and to ensure compliance."

Arms Control Activities of Foreign Nations

See pages 119-120 for abbreviations.

Nation	Membership in Alliances/ Groupings	Nuclear Status	Arms Control Accords to Which Party or Signatory
Afghanistan	IAEA NAM UN	--	LTBT OS NPT SEA BIO
Albania	IAEA UN	--	--
Algeria	ARAB IAEA NAM OAU OPEC UN	--	LTBT
Angola	NAM OAU UN	--	--
Antigua and Barbuda	--	--	OS LA NPT SEA GP ENV
Argentina	NAM OAS UN	Has most advanced nuclear program in Latin America.	ANT LTBT OS

Nation	Membership in Alliances/ Groupings	Nuclear Status	Arms Control Accords to Which Party or Signatory
(Argentina, cont.)	IAEA	Uranium enrichment plant under construction.	LA SEA GP BIO
Australia	ANZUS IAEA UN SEATO	--	ANT LTBT OS NPT SEA GP BIO ENV
Austria	IAEA UN	--	LTBT OS NPT SEA GP BIO
Bahamas	UN	--	LTBT OS LA NPT GP
Bangladesh	IAEA NAM UN	--	NPT ENV
Barbados	OAS UN	--	OS LA NPT GP BIO
Belgium	EEC EURATOM NATO UN	--	ANT LTBT OS NPT SEA GP BIO ENV
Belize	--	--	GP
Benin	NAM OAU UN	--	LTBT NPT SEA BIO ENV
Bhutan	NAM UN	--	LTBT GP BIO
Bolivia	IAEA NAM	--	LTBT OS

Nation	Membership in Alliances/ Groupings	Nuclear Status	Arms Control Accords to Which Party on Signatory
	OAS UN		LA NPT SEA BIO ENV
Botswana	NAM OAU UN	--	LTBT OS NPT SEA GP BIO
Brazil	IAEA OAS UN	Not a nuclear power but possesses know-how to develop nuclear weapons.	ANT LTBT OS LA SEA GP BIO ENV
Bulgaria	WP IAEA UN	--	ANT LTBT OS NPT SEA GP BIO ENV
Burma	IAEA UN	--	LTBT OS SEA GP BIO
Burundi	NAM OAU UN	--	LTBT OS NPT SEA BIO
Cameroon	IAEA NAM OAU UN	--	LTBT OS NPT SEA
Canada	IAEA NATO OAS (obs.) UN	--	LTBT OS NPT SEA GP BIO ENV
Cape Verde	NAM OAU	--	LTBT NPT

Nation	Membership in Alliances/ Groupings	Nuclear Status	Arms Control Accords to Which Party or Signatory
(Cape Verde, cont.)	UN		SEA BIO ENV
Central African Republic	NAM OAU UN	--	LTBT OS NPT SEA GP BIO
Chad	NAM OAU UN	--	LTBT NPT
Chile	IAEA OAS UN	--	ANT LTBT OS LA GP BIO
China	IAEA UN	Nuclear power	ANT OS LA GP
Colombia	IAEA OAS UN	--	LTBT OS LA NPT SEA BIO
Congo	NAM OAU UN	--	NPT SEA BIO
Costa Rica	IAEA OAS UN	--	LTBT LA NPT SEA BIO
Cuba	IAEA NAM OAS UN	--	GP BIO ENV
Cyprus	IAEA NAM UN	--	LTBT OS NPT SEA GP BIO ENV
Czechoslovakia	WP IAEA UN	--	ANT LTBT OS

Nation	Membership in Alliances/ Groupings	Nuclear Status	Arms Control Accords to Which Party or Signatory
Denmark	EEC EURATOM IAEA NATO UN	--	NPT SEA GP BIO ENV ANT LTBT OS
Dominica	OAS UN	--	NPT SEA GP BIO ENV OS
Dominican Republic	IAEA OAS UN	--	NPT SEA GP BIO ENV LTBT OS LA
Ecuador	IAEA OAS OPEC UN	--	NPT SEA GP BIO LTBT OS LA
Egypt	IAEA NAM OAU UN ARAB	--	NPT GP BIO LTBT OS NPT
El Salvador	IAEA OAS UN	--	GP BIO ENV LTBT OS LA NPT GP BIO
Equatorial Guinea	NAM OAU UN	--	SEA
Ethiopia	IAEA NAM OAU	--	LTBT OS NPT

Nation	Membership in Alliances/ Groupings	Nuclear Status	Arms Control Accords to Which Party or Signatory
(Ethiopia, cont.)	UN		SEA GP BIO ENV
Fiji	UN	--	LTBT OS NPT GP BIO
Finland	IAEA UN	--	LTBT OS NPT SEA GP BIO ENV
France	EEC EURATOM IAEA NATO SEATO OAS (obs.) UN	Nuclear power	ANT OS LA GP
Gabon	IAEA NAM OAU OPEC UN	--	LTBT OS NPT SEA GP BIO
Gambia	NAM OAU UN	--	LTBT OS NPT SEA GP BIO
Germany, East	IAEA UN WP	--	ANT LTBT OS NPT SEA GP BIO ENV
Germany, West	EURATOM IAEA NATO OAS (obs.) UN	--	ANT LTBT OS NPT SEA GP BIO ENV

Nation	Membership in Alliances/ Groupings	Nuclear Status	Arms Control Accords to Which Party or Signatory
Ghana	IAEA NAM OAU UN	--	LTBT OS NPT SEA GP BIO ENV
Greece	IAEA EEC NATO UN	--	LTBT OS NPT SEA GP BIO ENV
Grenada	NAM OAS UN	--	OS LA NPT SEA GP
Guatemala	IAEA OAS UN	--	LTBT LA NPT SEA BIO
Guinea	NAM OAU UN	--	SEA
Guinea-Bissau	NAM OAU UN	--	NPT SEA BIO
Guyana	NAM OAS UN	--	OS GP BIO
Haiti	IAEA OAS UN	--	LTBT OS LA NPT BIO
Honduras	OAS UN	--	LTBT OS LA NPT SEA BIO
Hungary	IAEA UN WP	--	LTBT OS NPT SEA GP BIO ENV

Nation	Membership in Alliances/ Groupings	Nuclear Status	Arms Control Accords to Which Party or Signatory
Iceland	NATO UN IAEA	--	LTBT OS NPT SEA GP BIO ENV
India	NAM UN	Minor nuclear power. Detonated nuclear device in 1974. Has technology and materials to make nuclear weapons.	ANT LTBT OS SEA GP BIO ENV
Indonesia	ASEAN IAEA NAM OPEC UN	--	LTBT OS NPT GP BIO
Iran	IAEA NAM OPEC UN	--	LTBT OS NPT SEA GP BIO ENV
Iraq	ARAB IAEA NAM OPEC UN	Iraq's nuclear reactor destroyed by Israel. Efforts to rebuild derailed by Iran-Iraqi war.	LTBT OS NPT SEA GP BIO ENV
Ireland	EEC EURATOM IAEA UN	--	LTBT OS NPT SEA GP BIO ENV
Israel	IAEA OAS (obs.) UN	Probably a nuclear power	LTBT OS GP
Italy	EEC EURATOM IAEA NATO OAS (obs.) UN	--	ANT LTBT OS NPT SEA GP BIO ENV

Nation	Membership in Alliances/ Groupings	Nuclear Status	Arms Control Accords to Which Party or Signatory
Ivory Coast	IAEA NAM OAU UN	--	LTBT NPT SEA GP BIO
Jamaica	IAEA NAM OAS UN	--	LTBT OS LA NPT SEA GP BIO
Japan	IAEA UN	--	ANT LTBT OS NPT SEA GP BIO ENV
Jordan	ARAB IAEA NAM UN	--	LTBT OS NPT SEA GP BIO
Kampuchea	IAEA NAM UN	--	NPT SEA BIO
Kenya	IAEA NAM OAU UN	--	LTBT NPT GP BIO
Korea, North	IAEA UN (obs.)	--	LTBT OS NPT SEA BIO
Korea, South	IAEA UN (obs.)	--	LTBT OS NPT SEA BIO
Kuwait	ARAB IAEA NAM OPEC UN	--	LTBT OS NPT GP BIO ENV
Laos	NAM	--	LTBT

Nation	Membership in Alliances/ Groupings	Nuclear Status	Arms Control Accords to Which Party or Signatory
(Laos, cont.)	UN		OS NPT SEA BIO ENV
Lebanon	ARAB IAEA NAM UN	--	LTBT OS NPT SEA GP BIO ENV
Lesotho	NAM OAU UN	--	OS NPT SEA GP BIO
Liberia	IAEA NAM OAU UN	--	LTBT NPT SEA GP BIO ENV
Libya	ARAB IAEA NAM OPEC UN	Has embryonic nuclear program. Trying to acquire nuclear capability.	LTBT OS NPT GP BIO
Liechtenstein	IAEA	--	NPT
Luxembourg	EEC EURATOM IAEA NATO UN	--	LTBT OS NPT SEA GP BIO ENV
Madagascar	IAEA NAM OAU UN	--	LTBT OS NPT SEA GP BIO
Malawi	NAM OAU UN	--	LTBT GP BIO ENV
Malaysia	ASEAN IAEA NAM UN	--	LTBT OS NPT SEA

Nation	Membership in Alliances/ Groupings	Nuclear Status	Arms Control Accords to Which Party or Signatory
Maldives	NAM UN	--	GP BIO NPT
Mali	IAEA NAM OAU UN	--	GP LTBT OS NPT SEA GP BIO
Malta	NAM UN	--	LTBT NPT SEA GP BIO
Mauritania	ARAB NAM OAU UN	--	LTBT
Mauritius	IAEA NAM OAU UN	--	LTBT OS NPT SEA GP BIO
Mexico	IAEA OAS UN	--	LTBT OS LA NPT GP BIO
Monaco	IAEA UN (obs.)	--	GP
Mongolia	IAEA UN		LTBT OS NPT SEA GP BIO ENV
Morocco	ARAB IAEA NAM OAU UN	--	LTBT OS NPT SEA GP BIO ENV
Mozambique	NAM OAU UN	--	--

Nation	Membership in Alliances/ Groupings	Nuclear Status	Arms Control Accords to Which Party or Signatory
Nauru	--	--	NPT
Nepal	NAM	--	LTBT
	UN		OS
			NPT
			SEA
			GP
			BIO
Netherlands	EEC	--	ANT
	EURATOM		LTBT
	IAEA		OS
	NATO		LA
	OAS (obs.)		NPT
	UN		SEA
			GP
			BIO
			ENV
New Zealand	ANZUS	--	ANT
	SEATO		LTBT
	IAEA		OS
	UN		NPT
			SEA
			GP
			BIO
Nicaragua	IAEA	--	LTBT
	NAM		OS
	OAS		LA
	UN		NPT
			SEA
			GP
			BIO
			ENV
Niger	IAEA	--	LTBT
	NAM		OS
	OAU		SEA
	UN		GP
			BIO
Nigeria	IAEA	--	LTBT
	NAM		OS
	OAU		NPT
	OPEC		GP
	UN		BIO
Norway	EEC	--	ANT
	IAEA		LTBT
	NATO		OS
	UN		NPT
			SEA
			GP
			BIO
			ENV
Oman	ARAB	--	--

Nation	Membership in Alliances/ Groupings	Nuclear Status	Arms Control Accords to Which Party or Signatory
	NAM UN		
Pakistan	IAEA NAM UN	Probably not a nuclear power as yet. Acquiring technology and materials to make nuclear weapons.	LTBT OS GP BIO
Panama	IAEA NAM OAS UN	--	LTBT OS LA NPT SEA GP BIO
Papua New Guinea	UN	--	ANT LTBT OS NPT GP BIO ENV
Paraguay	IAEA OAS UN	--	LTBT LA NPT SEA GP BIO
Peru	IAEA NAM OAS UN	--	ANT LTBT OS LA NPT BIO
Philippines	ASEAN IAEA UN SEATO	--	LTBT OS NPT GP BIO
Poland	IAEA UN WP	--	ANT LTBT OS NPT SEA GP BIO ENV
Portugal	IAEA NATO UN	--	LTBT NPT SEA

Nation	Membership in Alliances/ Groupings	Nuclear Status	Arms Control Accords to Which Party or Signatory
(Portugal, cont.)			GP
			BIO
			ENV
Qatar	ARAB	--	SEA
	NAM		GP
	OPEC		BIO
	UN		
Rumania	IAEA	--	ANT
	UN		LTBT
	WP		OS
			NPT
			SEA
			GP
			BIO
			ENV
Rwanda	NAM	--	LTBT
	OAU		OS
	UN		NPT
			SEA
			GP
			BIO
St. Lucia	OAS	--	OS
			NPT
			SEA
			GP
			ENV
San Marino	--	--	LTBT
			OS
			NPT
			BIO
São Tomé and Príncipe	NAM	--	SEA
	OAU		BIO
	UN		ENV
Saudi Arabia	ARAB	--	OS
	IAEA		SEA
	NAM		GP
	OPEC		BIO
	UN		
Senegal	IAEA	--	LTBT
	NAM		NPT
	OAU		SEA
	UN		BIO
Seychelles	IAEA	--	OS
	NAM		SEA
	OAU		GP
	UN		BIO
Sierra Leone	IAEA	--	LTBT
	NAM		OS
	OAU		NPT
	UN		SEA

Nation	Membership in Alliances/ Groupings	Nuclear Status	Arms Control Accords to Which Party or Signatory	
Singapore	ASEAN IAEA NAM UN	--	GP BIO ENV LTBT OS NPT SEA	
Solomon Islands	UN	--	GP BIO OS NPT SEA	
Somalia	ARAB NAM OAU UN	--	GP BIO LTBT OS NPT	
South Africa	IAEA UN	Probably a nuclear power	BIO ANT LTBT OS SEA	
Soviet Union	IAEA UN WP	Nuclear Superpower	GP BIO HOT NUC HS ABM SALT I SALT II TTBT PNE ANT	LTBT OS LA NPT SEA GP BIO ENV
Spain	IAEA OAS (obs.) NATO UN	--	LTBT OS GP BIO ENV	
Sri Lanka	NAM UN IAEA	--	ANT LTBT OS NPT GP BIO ENV	
Sudan	ARAB IAEA NAM OAU UN	--	LTBT NPT SEA GP	

Nation	Membership in Alliances/ Groupings	Nuclear Status	Arms Control Accords to Which Party or Signatory
Suriname	NAM OAS UN	--	LA NPT GP
Swaziland	NAM OAU UN	--	LTBT OS NPT SEA GP
Sweden	IAEA UN	--	LTBT OS NPT SEA GP BIO
Switzerland	IAEA	--	LTBT OS NPT SEA GP BIO
Syria	ARAB IAEA NAM UN	--	LTBT OS NPT GP BIO ENV
Taiwan	--	--	LTBT OS NPT SEA GP BIO
Tanzania	IAEA NAM OAU UN	--	LTBT SEA GP BIO
Thailand	ASEAN IAEA UN SEATO	--	LTBT OS NPT GP BIO
Togo	NAM OAU UN	--	LTBT OS NPT SEA GP BIO
Tonga	--	--	LTBT OS NPT

Nation	Membership in Alliances/ Groupings	Nuclear Status	Arms Control Accords to Which Party or Signatory
Trinidad and Tobago	NAM OAS UN	--	GP BIO LTBT OS LA NPT
Tunisia	ARAB IAEA NAM OAU UN	--	GP LTBT OS NPT SEA GP BIO ENV
Turkey	IAEA NATO UN	--	LTBT OS NPT SEA GP BIO ENV
Tuvalu	--	--	NPT
Uganda	IAEA NAM OAU UN	--	GP LTBT OS NPT GP ENV
United Arab Emirates	ARAB NAM OPEC UN	--	BIO
United Kingdom	EEC EURATOM IAEA NATO SEATO UN	Nuclear power	ANT LTBT OS LA NPT SEA GP BIO ENV
Upper Volta	NAM OAU UN	--	LTBT OS NPT
Uruguay	IAEA OAS UN	--	GP ANT I.TBT OS LA NPT

Nation	Membership in Alliances/ Groupings	Nuclear Status	Arms Control Accords to Which Party or Signatory
(Uruguay, cont.)			SEA
			GP
			BIO
Venezuela	IAEA	--	LTBT
	OAS		OS
	OPEC		LA
	UN		NPT
			GP
			BIO
Vietnam	IAEA	--	OS
	NAM		NPT
	UN		SEA
			GP
			BIO
			ENV
Yemen (Aden)	ARAB	--	LTBT
	NAM		OS
	UN		NPT
			SEA
			BIO
			ENV
Yemen (Sanaa)	ARAB	--	LTBT
	NAM		NPT
	UN		SEA
			GP
			BIO
			ENV
Yugoslavia	IAEA	--	LTBT
	NAM		OS
	UN		NPT
			SEA
			GP
			BIO
Zaire	IAEA	--	LTBT
	NAM		OS
	OAU		NPT
	UN		BIO
			ENV
Zambia	IAEA	--	LTBT
	NAM		OS
	OAU		SEA
	UN		GP
Zimbabwe	IAEA	--	GP
	UN		

Key to Abbreviations
in Foreign Nations Table, pp. 101–118

Alliances/Groupings

ANZUS	ANZUS Treaty (U.S., New Zealand, Australia)
ARAB	Arab League
ASEAN	Association of Southeast Asian Nations
EEC	European Economic Community (Common Market)
EURATOM	European Atomic Energy Community
IAEA	International Atomic Energy Agency
NAM	Nonalligned Movement
NATO	North Atlantic Treaty Organization
OAS	Organization of American States
OAU	Organization of African Unity
OPEC	Organization of Petroleum Exporting Countries
SEATO	Southeast Asia Treaty Organization
UN	United Nations
WP	Warsaw Pact

U.S.–Soviet Bilateral Agreements

ABM	ABM Treaty
HOT	"Hot Line" Agreements
HS	Agreement on Prevention of Incidents on and Over the High Seas
NUC	Agreement on Measures to Reduce the Risk of Outbreak of Nuclear War
SALT I	Interim Agreement on the Limitation of Strategic Offensive Arms
SALT II	Treaty on the Limitation of Strategic Offensive Arms
TTBT	Threshold Test Ban Treaty
PNE	Treaty on the Limitation of Underground Nuclear Explosions for Peaceful Purposes

Multilateral Arms Control Agreements

ANT	Antarctic Treaty
LTBT	Limited Test Ban Treaty
OS	Outer Space Treaty
LA	Latin America Nuclear Free Zone Treaty

NPT	Nuclear Non-Proliferation Treaty
SEA	Seabed Arms Control Treaty
GP	Geneva Protocol
BIO	Biological Weapons Convention
ENV	Environmental Modification Convention

Part IV
Bibliography

Selected Books

Bracken, Paul. *The Command and Control of Nuclear Forces*. Yale University Press, 1983.

Cockburn, Andrew. *The Threat: Inside the Soviet Military Machine*. Vintage Books, 1984.

Dunn, Lewis A. *Controlling the Bomb: Nuclear Proliferation in the 1980s*. Yale University Press, 1982.

Dyson, Freeman. *Weapons and Hope*. Harper and Row, 1984.

Fischer, Dietrich. *Preventing War in the Nuclear Age*. Rowman and Allenheld, 1984.

Glossop, Ronald J. *Confronting War: An Examination of Humanity's Most Pressing Problem*. McFarland, 1983.

Kerr, Thomas J. *Civil Defense in the United States*. Westview Press, 1983.

National Conference of Catholic Bishops. *The Challenge of Peace: God's Promise and Our Response*. A Pastoral Letter on War and Peace, May 1983.

Scheer, Robert. *With Enough Shovels: Reagan, Bush and Nuclear War*. Vintage Books, 1983.

Schell, Jonathan. *Fate of the Earth*. Alfred A. Knopf, 1982.

Talbott, Strobe. *Deadly Gambits: The Reagan Administration and the Stalemate in Nuclear Arms Control*. Alfred A. Knopf, 1984.

U.S. Congress

Committee on Foreign Relations, Committee on Foreign Affairs (Joint Committee Print). *Legislation on Foreign Relations Through 1982*, Volumes I and II, February 1983. *Legislation on Foreign Relations Through 1980*, Volume III, February 1981.

Committee on Foreign Relations, Committee on Foreign Affairs (Joint Committee Print). *U.S. Arms Control and Disarmament Agency 1983 Annual Report*, 1984.

U.S. House of Representatives, Committee on Foreign Affairs, 98th Congress, 1st Session. *Calling for a Mutual and Verifiable Freeze on and Reductions in Nuclear Weapons*, 1983.

U.S. House of Representatives, Committee on Foreign Affairs, 98th Congress, 1st Session. *Status of Mutual and Balanced Force Reductions (MBFR) Negotiations*, September 22, 1983.

U.S. House of Representatives, Committee on Foreign Affairs, 98th Congress, 1st Session. *Arms Control and Disarmament Agency Authorization for Fiscal Years 1984–5*.

U.S. Senate, Committee on Foreign Relations, 97th Congress, 2nd Session. *Nuclear Arms Reduction Proposals*, 1982.

U.S. Senate, Committee on Foreign Relations, 98th Congress, 1st Session. *United States–Soviet Relations* (S.HRG. 98–174, 2 parts) 1983.

U.S. Senate, Committee on Foreign Relations, 98th Congress, 1st Session. *Controlling Space Weapons* (S.HRG. 98–141) 1983.

U.S. Senate, Committee on Foreign Relations, 98th Congress, 1st Session. *Arms Control and Disarmament Agency Authorizations* (S.HRG. 98–8) 1983.

U.S. Senate, Committee on Foreign Relations, 98th Congress, 1st Session. *Outer Space Arms Control Negotiations* (Calendar No. 635 Report No. 98–342) November 18, 1983.

U.S. Senate, Committee on Foreign Relations, 98th Congress, 1st Session. *Nuclear Freeze Proposal* (Calendar No. 488, Report No. 98–276) October 24, 1983.

Library of Congress, Congressional Research Service, *Star Wars: Anti-satellite and Space-based Ballistic Missile Defense* (Issue Brief No. IB 81123) December 1983.

Library of Congress, Congressional Research Service, *Space Policy and Funding: Military Uses of Space* (Issue Brief No. IB 82117) December 1983.

Library of Congress, Congressional Research Service, *NATO Nuclear Forces: Modernization and Arms Control* (Issue Brief No. IB 81128) December 1983.

Library of Congress, Congressional Research Service, *European Opposition to INF Deployment* (Issue Brief No. IB 83174) December 1983.

Library of Congress, Congressional Research Service, *Strategic Arms Reduction Talks* (Issue Brief No. IB 82114) March 1983.

Library of Congress, Congressional Research Service, *Nuclear Arms Control: START* (IPO 226N).

Library of Congress, Congressional Research Service, *Nuclear Arms Control: INF* (IPO 227N).

Library of Congress, Congressional Research Service, *The Soviet Position in the Intermediate-Range Nuclear Forces (INF) Negotiations and Soviet Reaction to the U.S. INF Proposals* (84–501 S) Jan. 1984.

Library of Congress, Congressional Research Service, *U.S.–Soviet Negotiations to Limit Intermediate-Range Nuclear Forces* (82–136 S) July 1982.

Library of Congress, Congressional Research Service, *The Soviet Position in the Strategic Arms Reduction Talks (START) and Soviet Reaction to the U.S. START Proposals* (83–620 S) December 1983.

Library of Congress, Congressional Research Service, *The START Proposal: Verification Issues* (IP 226) June 25, 1982.

Library of Congress, Congressional Research Service, *Nuclear Freeze Alternatives,* Report #83–95 F, May 11, 1983.

Library of Congress, Congressional Research Service, *Nuclear Freeze: Arms Control Proposals,* April 11, 1984.

U.S. Executive Agencies

Arms Control and Disarmament Agency, *Documents on Disarmament, 1978, 1979, 1980.*

Arms Control and Disarmament Agency, *FY 1985 Arms Control Impact Statements,* 1984.

Arms Control and Disarmament Agency, *Effects of Nuclear War, April 1979.*

Arms Control and Disarmament Agency, *Arms Control and Disarmament Agreements, Texts and Histories of Negotiation,* 1982 Edition.

Arms Control and Disarmament Agency, *Special Report: 1980 Review Conference on the Treaty on the Non-Proliferation of Nuclear Weapons,* November 1980.

Department of Defense, *Soviet Military Power, 1984,* April 1984.

Department of Defense, *Continuing Development of Chemical Weapons Capabilities in the U.S.S.R.,* October 1983.

Department of State, Bureau of Public Affairs, *A Short Guide to U.S. Arms Control Policy,* October 1984.

Department of State, Bureau of Public Affairs, *Security and Arms Control: The Search for a More Stable Peace,* September 1984.

Department of State, Bureau of Public Affairs, *Realism, Strength, Negotiation,* May 1984.

Department of State, Bureau of Public Affairs, (Current Policy No. 587) *Negotiating with the Soviets,* June 1, 1984.

Department of State, Bureau of Public Affairs, *SALT II Agreement, Vienna, June 18, 1979.* Selected Documents No. 12 B, July 1979.

Federal Emergency Management Agency, *What You Should Know About Nuclear Preparedness* (pamphlet), November 1983.

Federal Emergency Management Agency, *This Is the Federal Emergency Management Agency* (pamphlet), May 1983.

Federal Emergency Management Agency, *In Time of Emergency, A Citizen's Handbook, 1983.*

General Accounting Office, *Information on ACDA's Personnel and Budget Levels and Related Matters,* GAO/NSIAD-83-63, September 13, 1983.

General Accounting Office, *Status of the Peacekeeper (MX) Weapon System,* GAO/NSIAD-84-112, May 9, 1984.

General Accounting Office, *Status and Reporting of Trident II System,* GAO/NSIAD-84-86, May 15, 1984.

General Accounting Office, *The Federal Emergency Management Agency's Plan for Revitalizing U.S. Civil Defense: A Review of Three Major Plan Components,* GAO/NSIAD-84-11, April 16, 1984.

General Advisory Committee on Arms Control and Disarmament, *A Quarter Century of Soviet Compliance Practices Under Arms Control Commitments,* 1958–1983.

The White House, *Report to the Congress, U.S. Policy on ASAT Control,* March 31, 1984.

The White House, *The United States Initiative to Ban Chemical Weapons,* April 18, 1984.

The White House, *President Reagan on Peace, Arms Reductions and Deterrence,* November 18, 1983.

United Nations

Committee on Disarmament, *Report to the General Assembly* (CD/421), Geneva, September 1983.

Disarmament Commission, *Report to the General Assembly,* New York, NY 1983.

International Atomic Energy Agency, *What It Is and What It Does,* Vienna, October 1981.

International Atomic Energy Agency, IAEA *Safeguards, An Introduction,* Vienna, 1981.

International Atomic Energy Agency, *The Annual Report for 1982,* Vienna, 1983.

United Nations, Department of Disarmament Affairs
  Fact Sheet 19: *The New Convention on Inhumane Weapons, A Summary*
  Fact Sheet 21: *Relationship Between Disarmament and Development, A Summary*

Fact Sheet 23: *Preparations for the Second Special Session on Disarmament*
Fact Sheet 24: *World Disarmament Campaign*
Fact Sheet 26: *U.N. General Assembly, Second Special Session on Disarmament.*
Fact Sheet 32: *The Sea-Bed Treaty. Results of the Second Review Conference of the States Parties.*
Fact Sheet 33: *Treaty on the Non-Proliferation of Nuclear Weapons. Review Conference of the States Parties, Geneva 1985.*

United Nations, Department of Public Information, *The United Nations Versus the Arms Race*, New York, N.Y., 1980.

United Nations, Department of Public Information, *The Arms Race or the Human Race? A Choice for Mankind*, New York, N.Y., 1981.

United Nations, Department of Public Information, *Final Document, Special Session of the General Assembly on Disarmament*, 1978.

United Nations, General Assembly, *Review of the Implementation of the Recommendations and Decisions Adopted by the General Assembly at Its Tenth Special Session*. A/35/257 May 23, 1980.

Nongovernment

The Arms Control Association, *Arms Control and National Security; An Introduction*, Washington, DC, 1983.

The Arms Control Association, *A Glossary of Arms Control Terms* (William H. Kincade and Jeffrey D. Porro, editors), Washington, DC, 1979.

The Arms Control Association and the International Institute for Strategic Studies, *Approaches to East-West Arms Control* (William H. Kincade, Nancy Yinger, and Gloria C. Duffy, editors), Washington, DC, 1979.

The Carnegie Endowment for International Peace, *Negotiating Security: An Arms Control Reader* (William H. Kincade and Jeffrey D. Porro, editors), Washington, DC, 1979.

Common Cause, *You Can Prevent Nuclear War*, Washington, DC, 1983.

Sanford Gottlieb, *What About the Russians?*, UCAM, Washington, DC, 1982.

The Riverside Disarmament Program, *The Arms Race and Us*, 490 Riverside Drive, New York, NY 10027, November, 1981.

Stockholm International Peace Research Institute, *Armaments or Disarmament?* Stockholm, 1983.

The Trilateral Commission, *Security and Disarmament*, 345 East 46th
Street, New York, NY 10017, February 1982.
Union of Concerned Scientists, et al., *Solutions to the Nuclear Arms
Race*, Briefing Manual, November 11, 1982.

Periodicals

Arms Control Today (published monthly by the Arms Control Associa-
tion).
Common Cause Magazine (published monthly by Common Cause).
Disarmament (published three times annually by the United Nations,
Department of Disarmament Affairs).

Selected Periodical Articles

Kenneth L. Adelman, "Arms Control With and Without Agreements,"
Foreign Affairs, Winter 1984/85.
McGeorge Bundy, George F. Kennan, Robert S. McNamara, and
Gerard Smith, "Nuclear Weapons and the Atlantic Alliance,"
Foreign Affairs, Spring 1982.
McGeorge Bundy, George F. Kennan, Robert S. McNamara, and
Gerard Smith, "The President's Choice: Star Wars or Arms
Control," *Foreign Affairs*, Winter 1984/85.
Daniel Deudney, "Unlocking Space," *Foreign Policy* No. 53, Winter
1983/84.
Randall Forsberg, "A Bilateral Nuclear Weapon Freeze," *Scientific
American*, November 1982.
Colin S. Gray, "Moscow Is Cheating," *Foreign Policy*, No. 56, Fall 1984.
Blaine Harden, "The Gassing of Washington," *The Washingtonian*,
February 1984.
Stanley Kober, "Swapping with the Empire," *Foreign Policy*, No. 54,
Spring 1984.
Michael Krepon, "Both Sides Are Hedging," *Foreign Policy*, No. 56,
Fall 1984.
George M. Seignious II and Jonathan P. Yates, "Europe's Nuclear
Superpowers," *Foreign Policy*, No. 55 Summer 1984.
John Steinbruner, "Arms and the Art of Compromise," *The Brookings
Review*, Summer 1983.
Tad Szulc, "The Unthinkable," *The Washingtonian*, June 1981.
Jonathan B. Tucker, "Gene Wars," *Foreign Policy*, No. 57, Winter
1984/85.

John P. Wallach, "A Walk in the Woods," *The Washingtonian*, January 1984.

Daniel Yankelovich and John Doble, "The Public Mood: Nuclear Weapons and the U.S.S.R.,"*Foreign Affairs*, Fall 1984.

Bibliographies

California Seminar on International Security and Foreign Policy, *Bibliography*, Santa Monica, CA, December 1983.

Center for International and Strategic Affairs, University of California, Los Angeles, CA, *Arms Control and International Security Working Papers*, Los Angeles, CA, (undated).

Center of International Studies, Princeton University, *List of Publications*, Princeton, N.J. 08544, September 1984.

Department of the Army, The Army Library, *Disarmament, A Selective Bibliography*, Washington, D.C., November 1981.

Department of the Army, The Army Library, *Nuclear War, A Selective Bibliography*, Washington, D.C., December 1982.

Department of the Army, The Army Library, *SALT, A Selective Bibliography*, Washington, D.C., August 1982.

Library of Congress, Congressional Research Service, *Nuclear Arms Limitation and the Effects of the Arms Race, An Annotated Bibliography*. Report No. 82-121 L, July 2, 1982.

RAND Corporation, *Arms Control, A Bibliography of Selected RAND Publications*, Santa Monica, CA, 90406, June 1983.

Stockholm International Peace Research Institute, *Publications, 1983–84*, Stockholm, Sweden, 1984.

United Nations, Department of Public Information
Fact Sheet 10: *Information Materials and Documents on Disarmament*, October 1980
Fact Sheet 29: *United Nations Information Materials on Disarmament*, June 1983.

U.S. Government Printing Office, *Disarmament and Arms Control, Selected Bibliography*, Washington, D.C., June 20, 1983.

Index